What People are Saying

"*Learning As I Go: Big Lessons from Little People,* is a sweet and endearing devotional that brings the joys of parenthood to the surface. In a day in time when many f  ons learned by and from their children as a 'problem into the crevices of your heart and bri those God places in our care, to the fo to us with the attributes of God and and purely teach us is just one gift from our Fath You'll smile, laugh out loud, and even sigh a few ahhh moments as Adams brings to light the sweetness of the Father, found in our children."

~Cindy K. Sproles
Award-Winning, Best-Selling Author,
What Momma Left Behind

"These days, parents need all the encouragement they can find. In her book *Learning As I Go: Big Lessons from Little People*, author Christy Bass Adams provides a plethora of inspiration. Her transparent writing leads all of us to view the world through a child's eye, leading us to both appreciate the kids in our lives and the amazing Heavenly Father who cares for us. This is definitely a book I'll keep on hand for gifts."

~Edie Melson
Award-Winning Author
Director of
The Blue Ridge Mountains Christian Writers Conference

"Being a parent is no easy job. In *Learning As I Go: Big Lessons from Little People*, Christy Bass Adams' masterful storytelling of unexpected moments with her children makes you chuckle while finding a godly perspective for your day."

~Beth Patch
Senior Editor/Producer for CBN.com

"Jesus said unless we become as little children, we cannot enter the kingdom of God. Christy Bass Adams shows us what this looks like through her devotional, *Learning as I Go: Big Lessons from Little People*. Prepare to be charmed."

~Lori Hatcher
Author of
Refresh Your Faith, Uncommon Devotions from Every Book of the Bible

"The devotions in *Learning As I Go: Big Lessons from Little People* are delightful and often laugh-out-loud entertaining. Christy Bass Adams has taken everyday occurrences with her children that we can all relate to and pulled out thought-provoking lessons for us adults. I especially liked the questions at the end of each devotion. A wonderful book."

~Debra L. Butterfield
Author of
Unshakable Faith Bible Study.

Learning As I Go

Learning As I Go
Big Lessons from Little People

75 Devotions for Parents

Christy Bass Adams

WordCrafts Press

Learning as I Go
Copyright © 2022
Christy Bass Adams

ISBN: 978-1-957344-22-5

Cover concept and design by Christy Bass Adams.

Published by WordCrafts Press
Cody, Wyoming 82414
www.wordcrafts.net

to Carter and Daniel
you will forever be my "sunshines"

Contents

Broken Tracks

God made my life complete when I placed all the pieces
before him. When I got my act together, he gave me a fresh start.
~Psalm 18:20 (MSG)

Daniel desperately tried to fix the broken track. He pushed and jammed but nothing made the pieces go back together. "Mama, I can't do it," he cried.

"Just bring it to me and I'll fix it." He pulled off a tiny piece of track and brought it to me.

"No, Baby. You need to bring all of the broken pieces to me."

He hurried back to the floor, gathered several other small, broken pieces, and set them in my lap. I hooked the pieces back together. "Now, bring me the bigger piece so we can hook it all back together."

He snatched the newly constructed piece out of my hand and tried to connect it to the main track on the floor. He grunted and pushed, but the pieces just wouldn't hook together. "Mama. Fix it. Pweeeze." Now he was desperate.

"Daniel, listen. I must have ALL the pieces. I can't fix the broken track if I only have a small piece. Bring everything to me, all at the same time." Slowly he brought the whole track to me, including the piece he snatched away.

I hooked the tracks together, and he smiled. "No more broken, Mama. All new."

Immediately, I thought of Jesus. Patiently waiting for us to bring our broken pieces. *"Just bring it to Me and I'll fix it."* I imagined Jesus holding out His hands, waiting for me to give those broken pieces over.

1

"No, Baby, you need to bring ALL of the broken pieces to Me."
All can be such a hard word.

"Precious One, listen. I have to have ALL of the pieces. I can't fix your brokenness if I only have a small piece. Bring everything to Me, all at the same time." I thought about all those broken pieces scattered in my heart. If I would only trust Him with each one, He could fasten me back together. But like my son, I give and then snatch it back.

"No more broken, Child. All new." That's what can happen when we surrender. No more broken pieces. Made whole. Made new. All because of Jesus.

What broken pieces am I holding onto that I need to bring to God today?

Wear Your Own Shoes

The LORD has made everything for his own purposes.
~Proverbs 16:4a (NLT)

I think I'm gonna need some help," my three-year-old said through humble, teary eyes. Somehow, he had made it all the way down the steps and into the yard wearing my husband's heavy work boots. The poor guy was pinned down by the weight of trying to fill someone else's shoes. I helped him up and explained that he had his own shoes to wear that were made for his feet; he only needed to go inside and get them. Still not convinced, I assured him that if he would at least try to wear his own shoes, he would see a huge difference in how he moved around.

As I carried my husband's heavy boots back inside, I realized I am often just like my son. I see someone else who is more talented, athletic, or academic and I wish I was more like them. Sometimes I catch myself downplaying my specific personality and wish I was more like someone else. Instead of honing, feeding, and fueling my God-given talents and abilities, I often wish them away and romanticize someone else's gifting. Every step I choose to take in those heavy boots gets harder and harder and, eventually, I end up falling on the ground, pinned down by the weight of my own unrealistic expectations, begging for help.

This is not living. We were never designed to live someone else's life. Each one of us is uniquely made and if we keep trying to be someone we are not, then sooner or later we are going to be down on the ground, just like my son, saying, "I think I'm gonna need some help."

Let's make sure we are wearing our own shoes. God has made each of us unique with very specific gifts and talents on purpose.

Am I dissatisfied with my place in life because of comparisons I'm making?

I Don't Want to Hurt God's Heart

The LORD observed the extent of human wickedness on the earth, and he saw that everything they thought or imagined was consistently and totally evil. So the LORD was sorry he had ever made them and put them on the earth. It broke his heart.
~Genesis 6:5-6 (NLT)

"What's it mean to follow Jesus?" my oldest son, Carter, asked.

"First, we acknowledge He died on the cross for our sins and decide we no longer want to live for ourselves. Then we choose to follow Him. That means we try hard not to sin anymore. Sin hurts God's heart." After sharing several examples of what sin might look like, the conversation shifted gears. The boys went back to playing superheroes and monster trucks in the backseat, and I turned the music on.

Without warning, my youngest, Daniel, clobbered his brother. I waited for it, knowing a commotion was about to break out in the backseat. But it never happened. I looked back at my oldest. He had pulled away and tucked himself tightly into the corner of the car.

"Is everything okay back there?" I asked.

"Yes," he nodded. "Mama, I really wanted to hit Daniel back," he paused and through thoughtful eyes continued, "but I'm just trying really hard right now not to hurt God's heart."

I was floored. How could this seven-year-old so quickly grasp a concept that many of us will never master in a lifetime? His sweet innocence made me wonder, *Am I trying not to hurt God's heart? Am I doing everything in my power to watch my actions? Am*

I stopping myself when the Holy Spirit nudges me way down deep or am I falling prey to old habits?

In what ways am I hurting God's heart through sin in my life?

"Holy" Pokey!

So give yourselves completely to God.

~James 4:7a (NCV)

I taught Daniel how to do the "Hokey Pokey" and he was a huge fan. At two years old, music and dancing are a big part of his world. As usual, he had his own take on the song. After we put our arms in, took them out, and shook them all about, he pointed his little, wiggly fingers straight up in the sky, turned himself around and yelled, "HOLY POKEY!"

At first, we laughed and kept putting different parts in and shaking them all about. Then he got all excited and yelled, "Whole-self in, Mama!" I jumped up and played along, but immediately my mind switched gears. *If I am REALLY going to play "Holy" Pokey, then I actually need to put my whole-self in. None of this left arm here or right foot there. It's all or nothing.*

And just like that, I was no longer singing a silly song with my two-year-old; I was doing business with the Lord. Daily, I play the real-life version of "Holy" Pokey, and I need to remember to put my whole heart in, my whole mind in, all my emotions in, all my decisions in, all my actions in, all my motivations in, and ultimately my whole-self in. I can't keep putting it all in and taking it right back out. I've got to put myself in, leave myself in, and let Jesus start shaking me all about.

As we go about our day, let's work on changing our tune just a little. *"Put your whole self in, don't take your whole self out, put your whole self in and let Jesus shake you all about. Let's do the Holy Pokey, let Jesus turn your life around. He's what it's all about! HOLY POKEY!"*

Am I putting my whole-self in and leaving it, or am I taking my whole-self out because of fear?

I Got You, Buddy!

All praise to the God and Father of our Master, Jesus the Messiah! Father of all mercy! God of all healing counsel! He comes alongside us when we go through hard times, and before you know it, he brings us alongside someone else who is going through hard times so that we can be there for that person just as God was there for us. We have plenty of hard times that come from following the Messiah, but no more so than the good times of his healing comfort—we get a full measure of that, too.

~2 Corinthians 1:3-5 (MSG)

We were working on a project in our backyard that required us to dig a giant hole which left a steep bank. Our two young boys were determined to climb that bank. Carter discovered how to climb it all on his own. Well, everything that big brother does, little brother wants to do. I walked by on the upper ledge and Daniel was down at the bottom desperately trying to climb up. I leaned over to grab him, but he wasn't tall enough to grip my hand.

"Mama. Can't reach," he moaned through tears.

Out of nowhere, Carter came up behind Daniel and pushed him from the bottom. There was no way he had the strength to lift him up the bank, but he tried. Slowly, Daniel climbed a little higher.

Then Carter wrapped his arms around Daniel and said, "I got you, buddy." Carter looked up at me and said, "Mama, help pull him to the top." By that point he was high enough for me to grab his little arms and pull him to the top.

All I could think about was the picture of Carter, doing everything in his power to lift his baby brother up out of the dirt. He knew he couldn't get him all the way up, but just that little boost was enough to get him off the bottom and into the reach of Mama, waiting at the edge.

It's similar to what we as Christians are called to do. There are people all around us that are stuck in deep holes or messy dirt. We need to do everything within our power to come alongside them or even push them from behind and say, "Hey, I got you, buddy." Then we lift them up out of the mud.

We may not be able to lift them all the way up, but just that little boost might be enough to get them off the bottom and into the reach of Jesus, waiting at the top.

How can I help those around me get out of their pits and lifted up to Jesus?

I'm Here! It's Me!

I am the vine, you are the branches; he who abides in Me and I in him, he bears much fruit, for apart from Me you can do nothing.

~John 15:5 (NASB)

Carter started waking up in the middle of the night and walking through the house to our bedroom hallway. He then stands at the entrance of our bedroom and calls, "I'm here! It's me!" If one of us doesn't answer, he calls until we wake up and invite him into our room. Once he has permission, he sails right up in the middle and roots out a spot that looks like it was left just for him.

In the wee hours of the morning, I heard that little voice. "I'm here! It's me!" I invited him in, and he climbed over my husband. "Mama. It's too little. I can't fit!" We shuffled around until he had enough room to spread out and get comfortable.

When I woke up the next morning, my first thought was of Jesus standing in the hallway of my heart beckoning to me. "I'm here! It's me!" It wasn't a feeling of a one-time invitation at salvation, but of a regular occurrence. Every day, in every situation, Jesus is waiting for the invitation to join us.

But it's more than just an invitation to come in. He wants to climb back into His rightful place in the middle of our lives. For some reason, though, His spot keeps getting smaller and smaller as we move more and more stuff in the way. Fear, worry, control, unforgiveness, excuses, heartaches, habits, addictions, faithless works- all of these begin creeping in until the spot that used to be the "rooted-out-just-for-Jesus-spot," in the middle of our lives, gets swallowed up by the "bed-hog" of self.

Every time I hear my son's sweet little voice, "I'm here! It's me!" I can't help but smile. And I see a mental picture in my mind of Jesus doing the same thing every day—standing, waiting, and calling out to me, "I'm here! It's me!"

May His spot remain open and ready, not cluttered with selfish junk I've left in the way.

Is Jesus' spot open and ready, or do I have junk that needs to be moved first?

Mama, Is He Going to Take You Away?

But when I am afraid, I will put my trust in you.
~Psalm 56:3 (NLT)

Mama, why are you pulling over?" Carter asked.

"Because there is a policeman with his lights flashing behind me."

Tears filled my five-year-old's face. "Mama, is he going to take you away?" My son became obsessed with safety after a presentation at school, so when the policeman walked up to my window and asked for my driver's license, Carter fell apart.

"I clocked you at 25 in a 15 MPH speed zone. I am only giving you a warning, but make sure you slow down in the future."

I thanked the officer and looked back at my son while I waited on my license to be returned. Big heaves started. "Mama, you don't have any drugs, do you?" I choked back a laugh.

"No, Baby. Mama doesn't have any drugs. There is nothing that Mama has done that would make that policeman take me out of this car. He is just doing his job because I was speeding."

More tears and heaves. "Mama, I had a really bad dream the police came and took you and Daddy away." More tears. "Mama, don't let the police take you and Daddy away."

"Baby, nobody is taking Mama and Daddy away. That was just a dream, and tonight Mama was driving too fast. Like when your teacher gives students a warning before moving their clip, that policeman was warning me before giving me a ticket."

All the way home, I noticed his fearful glances toward the speedometer. As we pulled into the driveway, I grabbed his hand. "Don't let your fear keep you from enjoying the ride. Mama might go over the speed limit but if all you do is watch the speedometer then you are going to miss everything else. Fear of doing something wrong or of bad things happening keeps us trapped. Don't be so afraid that you miss the fun."

In the moment, I realized who actually needed to hear that message. "Don't let your fear keep you from enjoying the ride."

Alright, God, I hear you loud and clear...

Am I letting fear dictate my direction?

Choose to Engage

Direct your children onto the right path, and when they are older, they will not leave it.

~Proverbs 22:6 (NLT)

Mama, how does Mickey Mouse go to the bathroom?" my oldest asked.

From his face, I could tell he was genuinely serious, so I worked hard to stifle the laughter. "Well, I suppose he has an outhouse behind the clubhouse," I replied. We laughed and came up with all the funny places Mickey Mouse might use the bathroom. It was a completely unproductive conversation that I could have written off.

But I didn't.

I chose to engage.

I chose to take a hiatus from my day job as an adult and be silly. I chose to challenge his busy little mind with more questions that would give him something to think about. I chose to joke and laugh along with him. I chose to think like a seven-year-old who likes to watch Mickey Mouse. We spun out puns and laughed at our ridiculousness. And we bonded over his silly little question.

One day, his questions won't be so silly anymore. One day, serious issues will burden his precious heart. And on that day, like today, my son needs to know that Mama will take the time to talk to him. When he asks me how to get to heaven and what it means to live like Jesus, he needs to know I will engage with him. When he asks about girls and tells me he has a crush, he needs to know I will listen to him and give sound advice. And when he messes up and doesn't know where to turn, he needs to know that Mama will be there to listen, love, and point him to Jesus.

I still don't know where Mickey Mouse goes to the bathroom, but I do know my son knows he can always come to me with anything that's on his mind. Life should never get so busy we neglect to stop and talk with our kids.

In what ways can I become more available to my children?

Try Something New

For I am about to do something new. See, I have already begun! Do you not see it? I will make a pathway through the wilderness. I will create rivers in the dry wasteland.
~Isaiah 43:19 (NLT)

When Daniel was a toddler, we lovingly referred to him as Baby Godzilla. He grabbed toys, ran through the house, and then threw them as hard has he could at whoever was in his way. If his brother was building with blocks, he knocked them down. Toys with wheels, he purposely rolled them off the table onto the floor. He was a handful, to say the least.

The summer he turned three, I was asked to be the preschool director for Vacation Bible School. I wrestled with letting Daniel join the preschool group, even though he was less than a month away from being three. I knew how he acted at home with his brother and the thought of that behavior at church bothered me.

That first night, I left him in the nursery, and he was miserable. The nursery volunteer brought him to me halfway through the night. Daniel couldn't breathe and was red-faced from crying. Once he calmed down, he watched the kids and wanted to join. He sang the songs, followed directions, talked to his leaders, played the games, and made crafts. The way he adapted blew me away.

As I watched him sing and dance his little heart out on that last night of VBS, I realized that sometimes we have to try new things. I had so many doubts and questions about whether Daniel was ready, but he totally rocked it. At home, he was a busy two-year-old, but when presented with the chance, he became a mature almost three-year-old.

I can learn so much from my little guy. If I don't take the chance, step out in faith, and trust Jesus, I will never know whether something is possible. I can make all the excuses in the world, but until I step out, there's no way to know what God wants to do with my little life.

How can I trust God more and step out in faith?

Stuck in a Rut

Commit everything you do to the LORD. Trust him, and he will help you.

~Psalm 37:5 (NLT)

We started down the driveway and hit the clay road. The first few curves were a little slick. As we rounded the corner at the end of the claypit, my car wiggled and wobbled. I slowed down but kept a steady pace. There was one more big hill around the last bend, so I couldn't stop now.

Everything was great until my front left tire hit soft clay on the edge of the road. As we slid sideways, I kept pressure on the gas, causing my tires to spin. Mud flew, smoke stirred, but the car didn't budge. I tried backing up, but the more I reversed, the closer to the bank my car got. Back and forth I rocked; only moving a few feet at a time.

Inches away from the embankment, my back tire finally caught hold of a firm piece of ground and I hit the reverse. When we reached our original starting point, I told my son that we needed to turn around and throw in the towel.

He looked at me and said, "One more time, Mama. Just go fast!" Well, what else was going to happen? Get stuck?

So, I backed up onto a solid section of dirt road and mashed on it! Through the wiggly ruts, up the base of the hill, through the soft clay; twisting, turning, and sliding we finally made it to the top. Celebratory cheers rang out as we threw our hands up in victory.

"See, Mama. You trusted me and we made it up the hill," my son said excitedly. "Just trust me, Mama."

In that moment, God tenderly stirred my heart. Those same, hopeful words that were spoken to me by my son were now being whispered to my heart. "Trust me. Trust me up this hill. Just trust me."

It's in those simple, unexpected moments, we hear from God. "Trust me. Just trust me." And we know, even in the chaos, that He sees, knows, and cares. Oh, that we could trust Him with all that we have.

Am I holding back any areas that God needs? Do I trust Him?

Yaya, Close Eyes

No one lights a lamp and puts it in a place where it will be hidden, or under a bowl. Instead they put it on its stand, so that those who come in may see the light.

~Luke 11:33 (NIV)

On a typical Sunday, my sons are in the children's building during the service and my parents attend an earlier worship service. This particular Sunday, for some reason, we were all together in the same service. Daniel, two years old, was standing in the chair between my parents holding their hands during the congregational singing. He was dancing and smiling, having the time of his life.

After the singing, our pastor began to pray, and Daniel became quiet and still. As our pastor paused toward the end of his prayer, a collective, hushed giggle came across the back half of the church as Daniel yelled at my mom, "YAYA! CLOSE EYES!"

The look on my mom's face was priceless. She had opened her eyes to check on Daniel during the prayer and he called her out in front of everyone!

As usual, my thoughts went a little deeper. Daniel watches us and is learning the right and wrong way to do things. He may not understand what prayer is, but he understands that it is a time where he needs to be still, quiet, and keep his eyes closed. We have done it enough that he is now learning to recognize prayer other places and not only at meals.

What I learned in that moment is my children are watching. Every action, attitude, and conversation is being carefully scrutinized by these little minds and hearts who are looking to us to show them how to live. Will they see enough faith to recognize unbelief? Will they hear enough truth to recognize lies? Will they see enough hope that they grow a heart for the lost? Will they know what's important by the example I set? I think I have some work to do, how about you?

What kind of example am I setting for my kids with my life?

Dada! Are You?

Search for the LORD and for his strength; continually seek him.

~1 Chronicles 16:11 (NLT)

As we were walking through the hardware store, my husband became enamored with something in the tool section, like always. After a few minutes of trying to stop my wiggly children from killing each other, I headed outside to the garden section.

The excited "oohs" and "aahs" of my two-year-old and six-year-old let me know that looking at the colorful flowers was a welcome distraction. After examining every flower, we came back in to find my husband.

Around every corner, Daniel leaned out, and yelled, "Dada! Are yoooouuu?" Finally, after looking down every aisle, we rounded the corner and Daniel's face lit up. "Dada! There. Dada!" We couldn't get there fast enough. As we approached, Daniel reached out, desperate to be held in his daddy's arms. Dada picked him up and cradled him close.

Daniel's sweet little voice echoing through the store made me think about how often I intentionally look for God. Regularly, I read my Bible, write in my journal, and take time to pray. I go to church each week and spend time with like-minded people. But those actions can become mere habit. How often do I lean out, look in every possible place, and desperately call out for my Dada? Am I truly using all my attention, energy, and focus to find my Father?

What if we walked through the store of life and looked down every aisle, actively calling out, "Dada! Are yoooooouuu?" I guarantee

Jesus would meet us. He would hear our call and invite us to join Him on the aisle where He is working. He would be waiting there with arms wide open, ready to cradle us close and show us His love.

Am I actively looking for God or is He a part of the day that only gets checked off my list?

Every Second Worth It

"Every good and perfect gift is from above, coming down from the Father of the heavenly lights, who does not change like shifting shadows."

~James 1:17 (NIV)

That quaking awakening. Everything in the room is blurry. My brain is desperately trying to pinpoint my location. My heart feels like it is going to beat out of chest. Slowly, I realize where I am.

Then the cry. The original reason I woke up in the first place. The sound that motivates a parent like nothing else. I run-walk across the wooden floor on my tiptoes, careful not to disturb any other members of the house. Once I get there, the crying has stopped. Maybe only a dream.

I stare. Watch him breathe in deeply. A huge smile spreads as I take in this unplanned moment in time. Lingering longer than necessary, I throw a thank you up to the King. *Thank you for allowing me to be his mom. Thank you for sharing such a precious gift with me.*

So many quaking awakenings. Precious sleep interrupted by a cry or a yell. Many trips across that creaky, wooden floor. Nights of lingering glances. Midnights and mornings spent listening, watching, and praying. And I would do it all again and again.

A heart completely full. A heart completely thankful. A wholly, satisfied, tired mama.

But it is all worth it. Every. Second. Worth. It.

Have I taken the time to thank God for my kids today?

Beeeeg Pooool!

Trust God from the bottom of your heart; don't try to figure out everything on your own. Listen for God's voice in everything you do, everywhere you go; he's the one who will keep you on track.

~Proverbs 3:5-6 (MSG)

Daniel, twenty-one months old, went swimming in a "beeeeg pooool" for the first time. The child is fearless. He climbed up the steps, ran over to where I was standing, held his finger up three times, and counted. "One, one, one, DOE!" Then he jumped, whether I was ready or not. Even though he had on a flotation-style bathing suit and a ring, he still scared me every time he jumped.

My personality is a bit more cautious than Daniel's and his boldness presents a new learning curve. He doesn't "look before he leaps," he acts now and deals with the consequences later. As I watched this fearless child repetitively scare the ever-living-hooey out of me, I realized he is confident because he wholeheartedly trusts me. He knows Mama is going to catch him when he jumps. He doesn't worry, overthink, doubt, or fear; he simply trusts, and he jumps.

Wouldn't life be so much easier if we would simply trust and jump? If we would trust that Jesus is our security and jump when He prompts our hearts? Can you imagine how much simpler life would be? What if starting today, we changed our thinking, ran up to the side of God's "beeeeg pooool" of life and jumped into His arms? What if we trusted He would catch us and guide us where

26

we should go? What a different life we would live if we totally trusted Him with everything!

What's keeping me from jumping into God's arms and trusting Him with everything?

He Wants My Now

"Give your entire attention to what God is doing right now, and don't get worked up about what may or may not happen tomorrow. God will help you deal with whatever hard things come up when the time comes."

~Matthew 6:34 (MSG)

I lost my cool. My kids were fighting. I was over-tired. When suddenly, this tyrannical, hollering maniac possessed my body and I felt like a fly on the wall watching some crazy woman fuss at my kids. It was not my best moment.

And then I saw his eyes. My son, who was just being a kid and fighting with his brother, was no longer getting fussed at for his wrongs—he was receiving my frustration from my hard week. My lack of time to myself. Missed moments in God's Word. Sleep deprivation. He deserved none of it.

In that moment, instead of stopping and apologizing to my son, I went into excuse mode. *I'm acting this way because I get up all night with the kids and don't sleep. My attitude will get better if I could only have a few minutes to myself. When they get older, maybe then I can have more time to do the things I love, and that's sure to help this rotten attitude.* Every excuse in the book came to mind, but the truth was that I was simply being selfish. I chose my anger and frustration over forgiveness and humility. I chose to be ugly.

But what I didn't see then that I see now is even when I'm a tyrannical maniac and I choose self over Jesus, God still wants me. He wants me now, just like I am. He wants my pajama pants and crazy hair. He wants my slippered feet and baggy eyes. He wants my aching joints and weary muscles. He even wants me before I've had my coffee (He's a brave soul!) and after I've reached my tired max for the day. If I will just stop and listen, He is wooing me. He has special things to tell me, sweet reminders of who He is and how much He loves me. He wants to spend time with me. Even when I make a giant fool of myself.

So, I apologized to my son. He looked at me like I had three heads, but I felt better afterward. And I stopped making excuses and made time to meet with God, even though it was scattered throughout the day. It's intentionality that leads to quality. He wants what I have to give. He wants me in whatever season I'm in. I just have to choose to choose Him.

What excuses am I using to keep me from coming to God just as I am?

Catch Me When I Fall

*The LORD makes firm the step of the one who delights in
him; though he may stumble, he will not fall, for the LORD
upholds him with his hand.*
~Psalm 37:23-24 (NIV)

Daniel turned a year old and is walking. Everywhere! He is climbing steps and going back down. He's absolutely fearless. Recently, we went to the playground, and he climbed right up the steps and walked between the barred walkways. Every time I reached out to help him, he pushed my hand away, determined to do it by himself.

Even though he was "doing it alone," I was either right behind, directly above, or immediately in front of him at all times. He was convinced he could do it by himself, but I knew he couldn't. There were too many unknowns and drop-offs on the side of the play yard. The steps were too steep. The hills were too high. The slides were too big. He had no idea what could happen if I let him do it all alone. Even though he kept pushing my hands away, when he stumbled, he always reached for me.

And my hands were always there to catch him.

As I was chasing him through the playground, looking like a giant she-ape with my arms out around Daniel, trying to anticipate which way he would fall, it made me wonder if that's how God feels chasing me through life. I change my mind and go different directions. I push God away, thinking I can do it on my own. I know what I want and when I want it and I have no idea what dangers are out there.

Thankfully God does for me what I did for Daniel. While I am trying to do life alone, He is either right behind, directly above, or immediately in front of me. He never takes His eyes off me. Even though I'm hard-headed and push Him away. Even though I try to make the climb all alone. When I stumble or fall, He's always there to catch me. I kind of like the idea of His big ole arms surrounding me on all sides like a giant papa bear, anticipating my next fall. And His hands are always there to catch me when I fall.

Am I offering my life to God or am I continually stiff-arming God, thinking my way is best?

Poop Happens

We can make our plans, but the LORD determines our steps.
~Proverbs 16:9 (NLT)

I had my evening all planned out. Drop the baby and four-year-old off at church and hide in my car for an hour. Stealthily, I walked the oldest to his class, careful to avoid eye contact. I know, this is not how it's supposed to work, but I was a tired, stay-at-home mom who just needed a few minutes to herself.

As I rounded the corner, there was a friend with outstretched arms, ready to take Daniel off my hip. I'd been spotted. But, the longer I lingered, the more I enjoyed the adult conversation, so I decided to stick around for Bible study. Daniel was passed around until he got fussy and as soon as he was back in my arms, I heard the explosion.

Quickly, I ran to the car as liquid leaked everywhere. My car was already a disaster, so Daniel's bottom half-rested on a crumpled sales paper while his head was lying in a pile of potato chip crumbs and chocolate pieces that fell out of Carter's booster seat.

I tried to get the onesie off, but the poop kept leaking and spreading. Finally, I realized there was no way to get it over his head without smearing poop everywhere, so I went for it. Patches of yellow above his eye and down his arm. Clumps of chunky yellow poop were all over his side and back. My hands and arms were covered and no matter how many baby wipes I used, I still found spots I missed on both him and me.

By this point I was laughing hysterically—that's all I could do. My poor kid had chips and chocolate stuck to the side of his head, poop streaks all over his body, and a sales paper stuck to his moist, little bottom. This definitely was not the quiet evening in the car I had hoped for.

But it was the evening God had planned for me. Sometimes our plans aren't His plans. We may get messy, but we have to trust that He is always in control, even when poop happens.

Is there anything I'm questioning right now that I need to trust God to handle?

Are You Ready to Listen?

Jesus replied, "But even more blessed are all who hear the word of God and put it into practice."
~Luke 11:28 (NLT)

Carter was being particularly hard-headed this morning and refused to listen to directions. I felt like a recorder that was set on repeat. "Carter, stop doing that," I said over and over again until I realized I was getting on my own nerves. Finally, as calmly as I could, I instructed Carter to go sit in his room until he could come back and listen.

I waited a few minutes and then asked, "Are you ready to listen yet?" I knew he would be tired of sitting alone and had to be ready to come back into the living room and watch his movie.

"No, Mama. Not ready yet." His response caught me off guard. He stayed in there a few more minutes, then I heard him bumbling around in the hallway. Slowly he sneaked around the corner and whispered, "I ready now." I smiled and invited him back into the room and we started over.

Then it hit me—I act just like my three-year-old. When God needs my attention, so often I'm "not ready" to listen. I have my own fears, worries and concerns that seem bigger than His leading. Other times His directions seem hard and might cramp my style. Like Carter, I throw my hands up, put on the brakes, and say, "Not ready."

But after a while, I set aside my stubbornness and peek back around the corner to see God still there patiently waiting. I smile and whisper, "I ready now," and we start over.

I'm so grateful for God loving me even when I'm stubborn. How about you?

Is there anything God is asking me to do that I keep saying, "Not Ready? Why?

Afraid of the Dark

God is light, and there is no darkness in him at all.
~1 John 1:5b (NLT)

Carter is scared of sleeping in his room. It doesn't matter if I leave the night light, a small lantern, or a flashlight on, there's something about the way the shadows dance around in the room that makes him fearful. When I was a kid, I was scared of the dark, too. I could play in my room all afternoon, but when the lights went out, it was a different story. It was like all my super-spidey senses came to life once I was alone in the dark. I could hear the tiniest creak, see the smallest flicker, and feel the faintest touch, even if it was just the air blowing past.

Darkness seems to bring out fear.

As I comforted my toddler one evening after dark, a question came to mind. What if being scared of the dark isn't such a bad thing? What if kids instinctively know that darkness is the opposite of light? What if being afraid of the dark is God's inborn nature luring us heavenward toward things of light?

I've pondered on this lately. As I have questioned, another train of thought has taken over: Am I doing enough as a parent, as a child of God, to make sure my son is more comfortable in the light than in the Dark? Am I instilling in him truths that will help him recognize the lies of darkness? Am I teaching him to trust in the light? Or am I setting an example of fear and cowering to the darkness?

I will never look at darkness the same, and I'm grateful to know the light who is always victorious over the darkness.

What am I doing to bring the Light, named Jesus, into my child's life?

Midnight Muncher

When I discovered your words, I devoured them. They are my joy and my heart's delight, for I bear your name, O LORD God of Heaven's Armies.

~Jeremiah 15:16 (NLT)

For his birthday, I made my husband a yellow cake with chocolate icing—his favorite. During his birthday week, he always leaves the cake out on the counter covered with foil and sets the fork inside the dish. This way, he can stop by anytime he pleases and eat his cake.

David woke up the next morning to get a taste, peeled back the foil, and yelled, "There was a mouse in my cake last night!" I hurried into the kitchen.

"He must have been a hungry mouse!" There were pieces of cake pinched off and crumbs scattered inside the cake plate. "Are you sure it was a mouse?" I asked as I looked for more evidence.

"It had to be. Neither one of us eats from all parts of the cake and leaves holes like that."

About that time, Carter walked into the room. His footed pajamas, face, and hands were covered in chocolate. "It sure was a big ole mouse. And here he comes for more!" David looked up and we both erupted in uproarious laughter. "And apparently that stool we thought he couldn't climb has gotten way easier!"

The sight of my 18-month-old covered in chocolate immediately brought to mind some questions. Am I waking up and seeking out God's Word before anything else? Am I so hungry for His message that the evidence of spending time in His word is all over my face?

When I wake up in the middle of the night, am I, like my son, a midnight muncher?

May we be so hungry for His word that the evidence is present all over our lives.

Am I actively seeking out time in God's Word before anything else in my day?

Oh, How He Loves Me

See how very much our Father loves us, for he calls us his children, and that is what we are! But the people who belong to this world don't recognize that we are God's children because they don't know him.

~1 John 3:1a (NLT)

I Am. Exhausted. We played with toys. Drew pictures. Made roads for his trucks. He danced. Crawled on the floor. Bounced like a frog over and over again. Used the chairs as tunnels for his trains. Colored the pages of my Sunday school book. He stood. Sat. Pulled my hair. Hugged too hard. He never stayed still for the entire two-hour praise and worship gathering. The kid wore me out.

During the first half, I was patient, trying my best to entertain a busy little boy while also singing and worshiping God. But as the second hour began, I could feel my irritation level rising. Just then, the band started the song "How He Loves". I picked Carter up and held him on my hip for the first part of the song. He was sweet and still until he decided he was done and wiggled right out of my arms.

Maybe I was at my limit. Maybe I really needed alone time with God. Maybe I needed a break. Whatever it was, my aggravation level reached its max. Just then, I heard the words to the chorus: *Oh, how He loves, yeah, He loves us, Oh, how He loves us, oh, how He loves us, Oh, how He loves.*

I looked over at my child, blue eyes beaming, dimples piercing his cheeks. He was having the time of his life. As I watched his curly hair flop back and forth with every bounce, I realized that

39

God loved me enough to give me the chance to have a son. Despite my failures, selfishness, and bad choices, He entrusted me with the care of a precious, silly, wiggly, little boy.

Finally, at that moment, true worship began. It seemed as if God was looking down on the whole evening, smiling, as He gave me that special reminder through a wiggly little boy and a song. "Oh, how He loves me" and keeps on loving me, not because of what I've done, but because of His great love.

What expectations do I need to set aside in order to truly worship God?

Broke Train

*This means that anyone who belongs to Christ has become
a new person. The old life is gone; a new life has begun!*
~2 Corinthians 5:17 (NLT)

We were getting ready to leave and Carter asked if he could
bring his "broke train" with him in the truck. Without batting an
eye, I told him he could. You see, in our house "broke train" is just
one of the many toys that Carter regularly plays with. In the beginning, he got frustrated that we couldn't get the battery to work. He
begged us to fix it and no matter what we tried, we could not get
the battery connection to fire properly. After a while, he stopped
asking for help to fix the train and accepted the fact the train was
simply broken. Soon he began to use it like it was without even
thinking about what it would be capable of if it worked properly.
Now, "broke train" is a toy that Carter carries around with him
everywhere, and the whole household has accepted "broke train"
just like it is.

As soon as I told Carter he could bring "broke train" with us in
the truck, my mind switched gears into life application mode. I
have accepted the fact that this toy is broken, so much so that it
is even in its name. If it was so easy to accept this broken toy, how
easy might it be to accept other "broken" things in my life without
batting an eye?

I have been thinking about this comparison all week long. So
many times I just write things off as, "Well, that's always been
hard for me and always will," or, "That's just the way I've always
been," or, "I can't beat that, I've tried already." When I do that, I'm

accepting those "broke trains" as reality; but even more, I'm not allowing God to be bigger than those "broke trains" that I carry.

It's okay for Carter to accept his "broke train" as it is, but for us, we need to examine areas a little closer, remove the labels of excuse, and ask God to begin working the brokenness out of our lives.

What sins have I allowed the label and excuse of broken? What can I do to fix that?

Grocery Store Perspectives

But the Lord said to her, "My dear Martha, you are worried and upset over all these details! There is only one thing worth being concerned about. Mary has discovered it, and it will not be taken away from her."

~Luke 10:41-42 (NLT)

In a weak moment, I allowed my three-year-old to push the grocery cart. He grabbed the handle and took the first corner like a miniature Mario Andretti. Me, in all my "mama-ness," grabbed the cart and brought it to a halt. I redirected, explained buggy-pushing rules, and we tried again.

And off he went at the speed of light. Once again I grabbed the cart, redirected, and explained the rules. Then came the crashing into poles and the speeding up and slowing down game where he dragged his feet. I just couldn't take it.

The cart pushing was once again my job and he was confined to the buggy until we reached the self-checkout counter. I asked him if he could control himself, and he nodded. As I was unloading the cart, faster than I could blink, he was on the self-checkout counter looking at me and smiling.

As I was about to blow my top and make him get down, he reached out and asked, "Can I hold your hand?" I stopped in my tracks. The story of Mary and Martha flashed through my mind. Mary, full of life, was content sitting at Jesus' feet while Martha was in the kitchen doing all the grown-up work and grumbling the whole time. Martha missed the moment.

I looked into my three-year-old's innocent, blue eyes. He had no idea why I wasn't as excited about buggy pushing as he was. He was having the time of his life.

"How about I hold all of you instead of just your hand?" I asked. He smiled, stood up on the counter, and leapt into my arms. I hugged him for a second, checked my attitude, and then confined the little hooligan to the shopping cart. Just because God was dealing with my heart didn't mean I felt like chasing him down.

But the encounter did change my perspective. And in the parking lot, I pushed the cart hard, hopped on, and we coasted to the car, giggling all the way.

What parts of life am I missing because I am being more of a Martha than a Mary?

My Little Parrot

*May the words of my mouth and the meditation of my
heart be pleasing to you, O LORD, my rock and my redeemer.*
~Psalm 19:14 (NLT)

My husband and I were riding around the farm with Carter this weekend. I ranted to David about something unimportant in the grand scheme of life. When I finished, I ended with, "Dern!" (I actually did just say "Dern!")

Without missing a beat, I heard this little voice echo from the backseat, "Dern!" Of all the words I had spoken, Carter chose this one word to repeat. I cut my eyes over to David, smiled a humble smirk, and immediately realized how impressionable my child was. He heard my ranting. He heard my tone. He heard my attitude. And he repeated my exclamation of disgust.

There are many things I cannot control in this world, but for the things that I can, I need to step up. I can control what I allow in my household. I can control what Carter watches on TV. I can control who we spend time around. I can control what books we read together. I can control what music we listen to. I can control my attitudes and actions. And I can control what I allow to come out of my mouth.

It reminds me of that little song we sang in church as kids, *"Oh, be careful little ears what you hear, Oh be careful little ears what you hear, For the Father up above, He is looking down in love, oh be careful little ears what you hear."* I'm so thankful for my little parrot and I pray that I can be a good sound to his little ears, not one that teaches him habits that are contrary to God's instructions.

It reminds me of that little song we sang in church as kids, *"Oh, be careful little ears what you hear, Oh be careful little ears what you hear, For the Father up above, He is looking down in love, oh be careful little ears what you hear."*

I'm so thankful for my little parrot and I pray that I can be a good sound to his little ears, not one that teaches him habits that are contrary to God's instructions.

What words, actions, and attitudes do I need to be more careful of teaching my kids?

My Kids Made Me Do It

I will give you back your health and heal your wounds,"
says the LORD.

~Jeremiah 30:17a (NLT)

W hen we were first married, my mom's gift to us was a box of handmade ornaments. Growing up, Christmas was a huge deal, so I couldn't wait to start our own, new family tradition. When December arrived, I excitedly decorated our first Christmas tree. Life was great. Christmas was joyful.

Fast forward two months to February 9, 2005. The phone rang at two in the morning. My parents and brother were at the hospital. My childhood home had been lost in a fire. Life stopped. Looking back, I can go directly back to that moment and see my joy heaped up in a pile of ash. Tradition. Home. Memories.

Everything changed. For five years I despised Christmas and only decorated a little Charlie Brown Christmas tree out of guilt. And then came my first son in July 2011. He brought such joy back into my life. His presence started healing the brokenness in my heart. As Christmas rolled around, I knew we had to put up a tree, if only for him. It was hard to decorate, but I made myself do it, even through tears. I am so glad we did because Carter was mesmerized with the lights and ornaments.

The next year, Carter began toddling and helped decorate. The following two years were easier and more joyful as Carter looked forward to Christmas just like I had when I was a kid. Then, Daniel was born in August 2015.

Our first Christmas as a family of four was the final turning point as I watched my four-year-old share the joy of Christmas with his baby brother. We sang and laughed. We picked out new ornaments for each member of the family. And we played Christmas music in the car during most of the holiday season.

That year, as I decorated our home for Christmas with the same box of ornaments (plus a few), my heart was full. And healed. It has taken a long time, but I can honestly say Christmas is one of my favorite holidays again. I'm so grateful that my kids made me do it.

What emotions are holding me back from enjoying special moments of life?

Sneak in Some Time

And if you search for him with all your heart and soul, you will find him.

~Deuteronomy 4:29b (NLT)

Confession time. Last night, I waited until the kids were in bed to bake brownies so I could lick the bowl and not have to share. I know, I'm such an awful parent. But seriously, that is my favorite part of making sweets, and there are just some days I don't want to share. Are there any other mamas like me out there?

I even had it so planned out that I left no evidence I had even baked brownies. Tell me that wasn't sneaky. But after I carefully cleaned the leftovers out of the bowl, I realized that if I went to such great lengths to plan and sneak in an evening of brownie making, then I obviously had the time and know-how to sneak in a daily time alone with the Lord. Talk about conviction.

So, I sat down, well after midnight, got out my Bible and read from God's Word. It wasn't boring. It wasn't hard to understand. As a matter of fact, it was exactly what I needed to hear that day and I am so grateful God used my selfish act to remind me of a sacred truth: I can sneak God in, too.

I did share my brownies with the boys. The guilt outweighed the pleasure of indulgence. But the lesson I am taking with me is I need to sneak in time for the Lord every day. And as good as that brownie batter was straight from the bowl, I need to remember that time with God is even sweeter.

What excuses about my time each day do I need to ditch in order to make intentional time with the Lord?

Exhausted and Grossed Out

"Let us not get tired of doing good, for we will reap at the proper time if we don't give up."

~Galatians 6:9 (CSB)

It was a hot, July afternoon and my five-year-old's bowels decided to move. I grabbed my almost two-year-old and the three of us ran into the unairconditioned bathroom. Of course, the public toilet was giant and my five-year-old began screaming and crying because he was afraid he would fall in. As I desperately tried to hold him up so he could do his thing, I saw my toddler wielding a plunger! "Look! Sword!"

Quickly, I let go of the five-year-old, who immediately screamed that he was going to be sucked into the giant toilet. I tried to retrieve the plunger from a very fast and wiry toddler. Finally, I pulled it from his hands. He laughed maniacally and began sliding, on the nasty floor, back and forth under the stall door. Now, mind you, my other son was still crying and moaning and sounded like a whale on a Greenpeace commercial. And all I saw were germs. Somehow I managed to retrieve my toddler and lift him up to the sink to wash his hands. As soon as we got them clean, I turned away to help my older son, and the toddler shoved his fingers in the drain on the floor and flexed his fingers back and forth.

I wanted to quit. Seriously. I was exhausted, grossed out, and done. But thankfully, every day isn't like this one and the good days usually outweigh the bad. I get tired. Sometimes I want to quit, but then I'm reminded not to grow weary in doing good. God will honor my efforts to be a good mom. He will hold me up and give me the strength to endure if I keep coming to Him.

It's all worth it in the end, even if I have to venture through a few gross bathrooms to get there.

What can I do to tap into God's strength this week?

Thankful for Underwear

"Give thanks in everything; for this is God's will for you in Christ Jesus."

~1 Thessalonians 5:18 (CSB)

I was fussing the other day about all of the laundry I had waiting for me at the house after work when an older lady said, "I sure wish I had laundry to do for others. My kids are all grown and live far off, my husband's gone, so it's only me. You best treasure that laundry while you still have it."

Frozen in my tracks, tears filled my eyes. I thanked the older lady and as I got in my car my whole perspective changed. I have two little boys at home who change clothes way too many times in a day and all their clothes are scattered through the hallway. But I also have two little boys who think that I hung the moon and stars. They still sit in my lap, even if I have to hold them hostage for a few minutes. They still give me hugs and kisses every day, even if I have to make them "pay the kiss toll" when they walk by. And they absolutely make my life more complete with all their stories and silliness.

When I got home that day, instead of grumbling and complaining while I did their laundry, I prayed for my boys. I thanked God for each of them and I asked Him to guide them in every step and decision they would have to make. I prayed for their salvation and future spouses. And instead of grumbling, I was thankful to God for that pile of clothes I had been dreading all day long. I was even thankful for the underwear.

What parts of my life am I taking for granted? What do I need to stop and say thank you for?

The Hug

Everyone should look out not only for his own interests,
but also for the interests of others.

~Philippians 2:4 (CSB)

One winter afternoon when my oldest was barely walking, we visited a new neighbor for the first time. They are lovely people and have every kind of farm animal you could think of. My son was instantly drawn to their tiny Shetland pony. After much hesitation on my part, I finally conceded and let him ride the small horse, with help of course. His face lit up like Christmas. I'd never heard him laugh so much or seen him smile so big. When he finished, I asked Carter to lean in and give our neighbor a hug. He reached out, wrapped his arms fully around her neck, and gave her the biggest hug he could muster. When he pulled away, tears welled up in my neighbor's eyes. That hug meant more to her than I could have ever imagined.

That little gesture totally changed my neighbor's day. My son taught me so much through that simple, heartfelt hug—show people how much they mean to you. It's that simple.

Sincere, intentional gestures can change another person's world for the better. Maybe it's a phone call. Maybe a text. Maybe a hug. Maybe a note or flowers. Whatever random or ordinary act runs through our minds this week, let's not ignore it. We need to act on it and give someone else a simple blessing, just like my son's hug. We may never know how God can use our small acts of obedience to help someone else. It might just make someone's day!

What opportunities do I need to take advantage of in order to bless those around me?

The Lonely Slide

*Just as each one has received a gift, use it to serve others,
as good stewards of the varied grace of God.*
~1 Peter 4:10 (CSB)

Mama, why is that slide on its side over there? Is it broken?
Why can't I play on it?" Every morning for a month, my son
asked me about the slide. It was in the very back section of his
school, in the broken equipment zone. The slide appeared to be
in perfect condition, which made me wonder why it ended up
tossed aside. Why not find a way to use the slide on another piece
of equipment?

As we daily talked about the slide, I thought about how many
people are in the spiritually broken zone. There are many believers
who have perfectly good talents, abilities, and gifts, and yet they
have stopped using them. For whatever reason, they have parked
themselves in the broken equipment zone.

Maybe they were offended or mistreated. Maybe they were
told that they had nothing to offer. Maybe they got tired or over-
loaded. Maybe other responsibilities got in the way. Or maybe they
convinced themselves they were no good and stopped offering
themselves to God.

Can you imagine with me what joy that slide used to bring when
it was attached to the playground? Can't you just see the faces of
the smiling children as the slide fulfilled its designed purpose?
Imagine with me what these folks used to be like, too. Can you
imagine what it was like when they were serving in their gifting?
Oh, what joy they shared with those around them when they were

attached to the Body of Christ and serving wholeheartedly. Can't you see the smiles as they fulfilled their designed purpose?

"I don't know why the slide is not being used, Daniel. But I wish it was on the playground. It sure has a lot to offer."

And so do we. Those old gifts, talents and abilities might be a little rusty, but there's someone somewhere who could benefit from their use. Volunteer. Pick up that instrument. Build a ramp. Cook a meal. Write a card. Connect with a body of believers. Let's offer our gifts and talents back to God.

What gifts and talents have I been holding back that I can offer to God for His kingdom use?

You Are My Sunshine

"In the same way, let your good deeds shine out for all to see,
so that everyone will praise your heavenly Father."
~Matthew 5:16 (NLT)

One of my greatest joys is listening to my boys sing. Carter enjoys singing, but Daniel absolutely loves it. Often, he will be singing in the back seat and out of nowhere he will point at me and say, "Hit it, Mama!" So, I jump in and pick up wherever he left off.

Lately we have been singing "You Are My Sunshine". One afternoon, after we sang a very silly rendition, Daniel asked, "Are me and Carter your sunshines, Mama?"

I smiled, "Yes, you and Carter are my sunshines. And Daddy, too." Daniel smiled and went back to singing.

Tonight, as I was drying him off after bath time, Daniel grabbed both my cheeks and said, "Mama, you are MY sunshine." I couldn't help but smile from the inside out as I hugged my sweet little boy.

As parents, we truly can be the sunshine in our children's lives. We can show them Jesus in so many ways. We can come home happy, joyous and overflowing with hugs and kisses, even when we have a bad day. We can choose to stop and listen to the same story for the eighteenth time with a smile on our face. We can play trains, drink tea, wear a crown, drive a race car, or have a dinosaur fight one more time. We can even sit down and listen to all the drama that is going on in our teenager's world with focused intention. We can make a choice to leave our cloudy day at the door and be the sunshine to the ones we love. I'm grateful that I can always share God's sunshine with my children.

Learning As I Go

Do the ones I love know they are my sunshines?

Falling Tree

This is my command—be strong and courageous! Do not be afraid or discouraged. For the LORD your God is with you wherever you go."

~Joshua 1:9 (NLT)

My husband walked in and proclaimed, "Let's go cut down a tree." So, the boys and I loaded up in the truck to watch. David plowed a trail to the tree with his bulldozer while the boys and I followed behind.

As David cranked his chainsaw, I leaned down to my sons and instructed, "Keep an eye on the tree. Daddy is cutting it carefully and it will most likely fall away from us, but if it suddenly twists on the stump, I want you to run really fast down the hill."

I turned my attention back to the tree and caught movement out of the corner of my eye. Carter had already started running down the hill. The idea of the giant tree falling on us terrified him and he didn't want to take any chances. My youngest, however, was "oohing" and "ahhing" as the tree started to sway.

My husband kept sawing and soon, the tree began to fall, exactly where he anticipated it would. My youngest son was amazed as he watched the tree crash to the ground. He soaked in the moment and enjoyed the thrill. Once the coast was clear, Carter ran back up the hill to see the tree. From where he was standing, he only heard the commotion, but did not actually witness the tree hitting the ground. The boys immediately climbed and ran back and forth on the fallen trunk.

As my husband hooked the fallen tree to the dozer and we backed out of the woods, I thought about the way my boys watched that tree fall. One kid was living in the moment, heeding instruction, but still participating in the event. The other one ran to safety, afraid of the what-ifs, and missed the whole thing.

As usual, God started working on my heart. When I see God begin to shake things up, how do I respond? Do I stand confident in His ability and watch Him perform His wonderful will, or do I run away scared, too afraid of the what-ifs, and miss the whole show? I need to take a chance. Live a little. Stop wringing my hands. And not be afraid to be a part of God's falling trees.

In what ways do I need to work on experiencing God more fully and not running away in fear?

The Eyes of a Child

"I tell you the truth, unless you turn from your sins and become like little children, you will never get into the kingdom of God."

~Matthew 18:3 (NLT)

The first time I took my oldest son to a park, I watched him soak in the sights. Everything was new and exciting. Within just a few minutes, an older boy began playing with my son. He was probably ten years old. I watched a few minutes and realized he had an obvious disability. At first, I wanted to jump in. *How dare that older child hone in on my son. He was too old to be playing with a two-year-old.* Thankfully, however, I refrained and realized that this sweet young man was experiencing this park adventure just as my son was—with fresh, excited eyes.

Soon, the older boy went home, and several younger kids showed up. Carter was running and playing. They chased each other and laughed, not once realizing they all had skin that was different than their own. After a while, the other kids left and Carter sat down to eat a snack. "Mama, I play friends," he said.

I smiled. He has always called other kids his friends, even if he barely knows them. I asked him, "Which friend did you like playing with the most?" I waited and honestly expected him to describe the kids by skin color.

"Friend in blue shirt," he replied.

Friend in blue shirt. Not black, white, brown, or yellow. He didn't see it. He saw other kids. He saw friends. He just wanted to have fun playing. Maybe that's why Jesus tells us, "Unless you turn from your sins and become like little children, you will never get into the kingdom of God." Children somehow understand the bigger picture and they love beyond the confines of color, disability, or personality.

"I'm glad you had so much fun with your new friends today," I replied to my son. *And I'm grateful for the innocence of children to remind us of the way we are supposed to love and care for one another,* I thought to myself. May God help us navigate this world, seeing everything through the innocent eyes of a child.

In what ways do I need to start viewing the world through the eyes of a child?

She Treasured These Things in Her Heart

And His mother treasured all these things in her heart.
~Luke 2:51b (NASB)

J ust as Mary, Jesus' mother, stopped and treasured those special moments, I couldn't help but think about the special moments that I have stopped and tucked away in my own heart over the years.

I held his tiny body against my chest for the first time, and I treasured this moment in my heart.

My son slept through the night for the first time and nearly scared me to death, and I treasured this moment in my heart.

He took his first step without my help, and I treasured this moment in my heart.

We had ice cream for the first time and his face lit up like Christmas, and I treasured this moment in my heart.

He went to the nursery today and cried for Mama, but I stood around the corner wiping away tears until I heard him playing, and I treasured this moment in my heart.

He pooped in the potty for the first time and I hollered, "Thank you, Jesus," and I treasured this moment in my heart.

He waltzed into his first day of pre-k and never looked back, and with tears, I treasured this moment in my heart.

He kissed his new brother on the forehead and hugged him, and I treasured this moment in my heart.

He said, "I love you," for the first time, and I treasured this moment in my heart.

He was reading his Bible just for fun, and I treasured this moment in my heart.

I ran my fingers through his hair, whispering a prayer as he fell asleep in my lap, and I treasured this moment in my heart.

I listened to countless story plots involving superheroes and villains, and I treasured this moment in my heart.

They are both laying here sleeping while I am typing, and I am listening to them breathe, and I'm thankful as I tuck another treasure deep into my heart.

Thank you, Lord, for the blessing of my children, and for all of the treasures you have allowed me to store up in loving them.

Am I slowing down enough to cherish these special moments with my children?

Let Someone Else Reel It In

*But those who exalt themselves will be humbled and those
who humble themselves will be exalted.*
~Matthew 23:12 (NLT)

My husband and I love to fish. One day, early in our marriage,
we were on the water and suddenly we found a pocket of trout.
I say we. It wasn't we. It was David. He found a pocket of trout
and brought in fish after fish. I cast my line in the same place
and the fish took his bait instead of mine. I reeled like David. I
even held my mouth crooked trying to be like him, but nothing
took my bait.

So, I pouted. I sulked. I crossed my arms and acted like I was a
toddler. David finally felt sorry for me and we traded poles. First
cast into the water and David landed another trout. On my pole.
Boy, was I hot! This competitive girl lost her cool, threw her pole
down, and quit.

Fast forward. We took our boys down the river and found a nice
sand bar. Another family with kids was there and their son wanted
to catch a fish. I told him the next fish I hooked, he could reel it
in. Soon, I called him over and he excitedly reeled in the fish. He
grabbed it and ran over to show his parents. My sons were next in
line, so I baited the hook to help them, too.

A lot has changed over the years. I used to want all the glory. I
put in the hard work of baiting and casting. I waited and when a
fish took the bait, boy was I excited to show it off. But now, I'm
content letting someone else reel it in. I don't mind putting in the
time and waiting on the fish to take the bait. I don't mind handing

over the reel and letting someone else get the credit. The smile on the kid's face, the pride that my sons felt—it's all worth it.

The same goes for grown-up life. It's not about getting the victory or earning the reward. God getting all the glory is what really matters; and when we do it for Him, we know all the hard work was worth it.

Am I more worried about getting the glory or am I doing everything for God's glory?

Hold Your Kids

And do everything with love.
~1 Corinthians 16:14 (NLT)

Tonight was the first night in eight years that David didn't have one of our boys sitting with him and falling asleep in his lap. Eight years. How did that even happen? He held Carter every night until the summer before he started school. About that time, Daniel was born, and he took over Carter's spot. And now, Daniel turns four tomorrow, starts pre-kindergarten next week, and Carter begins third grade. It's going by too fast.

And yes, I know what all of the experts say and I've heard all of the "dangers" of rocking our kids to sleep. But neither one of us would trade one single snuggle for the approval of some researcher who said it wasn't healthy. Phooey on research. We choose to hold our kids.

We choose to hold them in the morning when they want a quick snuggle before work or in the afternoon while they are watching cartoons. We choose to hold them after supper and listen to music together or in the wee hours of the morning when they crawl into our bed. We choose to hold them when they are happy and glad or sullen and sad. Every day, no matter what, we choose to hold our kids.

I know that soon the day will come when my boys will seemingly be too old to sit in our laps and let us hold them; but I sincerely hope they never realize it. I don't care if they are four, fourteen, or forty, our laps will always be ready, our arms will always be out-stretched, and our hearts will always be open.

These little boys have taught me the importance of making time and making room. We only have one chance with these little ones. I pray that I can honor God by giving it all that I have.

Am I taking time to hug and hold my kids every day?

Sitting On A Limb

A little yeast works through the whole batch of dough.
~Galatians 5:9 (NIV)

Dada, what are you eatin'?"

"Sunflower seeds. You wanna' taste?"

"Ew. That's for birds," Daniel paused a minute. "No, wait. Sure. I want a taste."

My husband broke the hull and handed my youngest the tiny seed. He held it. Then he tried to squeeze it. "Ouch! It's sharp," he exclaimed as he poked the pointy end. "I can't eat this. It will cut open my insides."

I laughed. "Daniel, it just feels sharp. Once you bite it, the seed breaks apart and tastes yummy. Give it a try."

He finally tasted it and wanted more. After he ate a couple, my husband jumped in, "Now, be careful, Daniel. If you eat too many seeds you might end up sitting on a limb and pooping on cars." We all laughed.

Later that same day, Daniel piped up from the back seat, "I want some more of those seeds so I can sit on a limb and poop like a bird." We all laughed hysterically, but his simple and silly statement made me think.

When Daniel first encountered the seed, he was hesitant, skeptical even. He carefully examined this new item that was potentially entering inside of him. When he thought about how sharp the edge seemed, he even feared the seed would cut him from the inside. He was careful about what he chose to put inside of him; but that isn't always the case.

So often we are lured and tempted by a new seed. It all seems great. Maybe we examine it closely, like Daniel did, but more often than not, we simply partake without considering the risks that the seed may bring. We watch violence on TV without batting an eye. We participate in gossip and slander. We listen to music laced with sexual imagery and suggestions. And we swallow each seed without even a moment's hesitation. If we don't stop and take the time to examine the seeds we are eating then we are going to be the ones sitting on a limb, pooping on all the cars, leaving a messy trail wherever we go. What goes in always comes out.

What am I allowing into my life that is eventually going to come out and leave a mess in my wake?

Learning How to Fall

If you think you are standing strong, be careful not to fall. The temptations in your life are no different from what others experience. And God is faithful. He will not allow the temptation to be more than you can stand. When you are tempted, he will show you a way out so that you can endure.
~1 Corinthians 10:12-13 (NLT)

Recently, I built monkey bars for the boys. Carter could hardly wait to try them out. He nervously climbed up the ladder, grabbed the first bar, reached for the second, and fear set in. His feet kicked and he begged for someone to catch him. We told him to calm down and relax his legs so they would hang straight down. He needed his feet closer to the ground so he could turn loose and fall without hurting himself.

He finally let go and he did not fall gracefully; instead he landed on his arm and wanted to quit. I told him he wasn't going to quit until he could learn to stop being afraid of the fall. After several nervous episodes and less than graceful landings, he finally learned to extend his legs, relax, and fall straight down, landing on his feet.

Navigating through life is like those monkey bars. We are going to fall, but we can't be afraid of falling. Falling is where we learn humility, experience weakness, and realize we truly are in need of God and other people He puts in our lives. It's the place where we become aware of our limits, put new safeguards in our lives, and experience the passageway of perseverance. Oftentimes falling is how we gain the definition for the rest of our lives.

We can't be afraid to fall, but we should be afraid of letting the fall define the course of the rest of our life. We need to get up, run the race, and try again. After a while, the falls will become less and less, and soon, we will make it all the way across the monkey bars.

Sometimes, though, the falls are bigger than we can handle— addiction, depression, and anxiety to name a few. In those cases, we need to seek help, or we will never make it across the monkey bars ourselves.

Do I know how to fall, get back up, and try again?

Turtles and Tetrazzini

*For God has not given us a spirit of fear and timidity, but
of power, love, and self-discipline.*
~2 Timothy 1:7 (NLT)

Mama, there's a turtle in the road! Stop the car!" my oldest yelled
from the backseat. Both boys and my husband leapt out and chased
the streaky head turtle. Each kid took a turn trying to grab it. Just
when they were about to touch him, the turtle moved, and the
boys spooked. Getting up the nerve to finally commit and grab
the turtle was just too scary.

Something similar happened at supper. Tetrazzini was on the
menu and it was a new dish for the boys. They both ate their fruit
but put off tasting the pasta until last. The idea of trying something
new was just too much.

Both situations proved to be harmless in the end. They each
finally got up the nerve and grabbed the turtle, held him, and
laughed as he kicked his feet around in circles. The tetrazzini was
a win, and both boys cleaned their plates. Once they got past the
newness and changed their mindset, they were able to muster up
the courage to try something new.

We all have experience with turtles and tetrazzini, don't we?
Change starts to come. New things happen. Questions linger. And
we freeze. What's going to happen if we grab that turtle? Will it
be a safe move? What will happen if we try the tetrazzini? Will it
truly be the best decision? And like my boys, we hesitate. The idea
of trying something new is often too scary.

Whatever new thing we are facing, we must be brave and do it.

Just because something is new doesn't mean it will be bad. Let's take a deep breath, set our worries aside, and grab that turtle with everything we've got. And while we're at it, let's eat that whole plate of tetrazzini, too.

Is fear keeping me from trying new things?

Distractions

We do this by keeping our eyes on Jesus, the champion who initiates and perfects our faith.

~Hebrews 12:2 (NLT)

Monday was one of those days. The kids loaded up for school and my car wouldn't start. I popped the hood and struggled for ten minutes to unhook the latch. Once I finally got it open, I asked Google where the battery was located. Thankfully, Papa came to the rescue and jumped the battery.

I made it to school by 8:30, and work by 9:00. As I was leaving for lunch, I noticed my tire looked low and that's when I spotted the nail. The rest of the afternoon was spent coordinating kid's school pick-up and grocery shopping all while my car was in the shop.

When we finally made it home, I hurried to the restroom. As the toilet flushed, the water raised all the way to the top. Of course it was stopped up. I watched and thought it would slowly seep down like always, so I left it and ventured to the main part of the house to help the boys with homework. Several hours later, I walked to the back of the house and stepped in a puddle of water. *Great,* I thought, *the pump is bad on the washer again.* As I made my way through the hall, I quickly realized it wasn't the pump.

The entire master bedroom, bathroom, and laundry areas were covered with an inch-deep layer of water. I took off my shoes and socks, rolled up my pants, and sloshed my way back to the bathroom. That's when I heard it. The culprit behind the mess—that stopped up, running toilet.

David ran outside to find the shop vac. I put towels down

74

everywhere and heaved things on the porch. I also grabbed the broom and swept the water toward any outside opening I could find.

When I finally sat down, my son asked, "Mama, what's for supper?"

"Supper?" I asked. "Well, that's a really good question. I do have to feed you, don't I?"

Distractions take us away from the most important things in life. What else had I missed that day because I was consumed with my own problems?

Do the everyday distractions of life take my eyes off you, God?

We Are Legos

The faithful love of the LORD never ends! His mercies never cease. Great is his faithfulness; his mercies begin afresh each morning.

~Lamentations 3:22-23 (NLT)

I was that kid who loved Legos. My brother and I had a gym bag filled with every shape, size, and variety of Lego, and we carried the bag with us everywhere. We made boats, spaceships, forts, airplanes, and anything else we could imagine and create.

Both of my boys have now discovered the joy of building with Legos. Last week, my youngest was building a fort and his tub of Legos was getting low. "Mama, I want to build a spaceship, too, but the Legos are almost gone."

I smiled, "Daniel, do you know what is great about Legos? Today you can have a fort and tomorrow you can take it apart and build a spaceship. You can start over every day and build something new."

As his face lit up with this new knowledge, I recognized that there was a much deeper truth buried in this simple conversation. Just because I build a boat today and get rocked and blown from here to there, that doesn't mean I have to build a boat tomorrow. Tomorrow, I can build a spaceship and rise high above the uncertain waves. Or I can build a fort with high walls and an open roof that will keep out the negativity, but still let in the Light. Or maybe I want to build an airplane and soar freely, with joy, making the most of my day. Each day is a fresh start, overflowing with God's new mercies, and just because yesterday was an utter failure doesn't mean that today has to be that way, too.

Let's not get stuck in what we think the day seems to be. We can start fresh and build our day on the foundation of Christ where newness abounds.

What obstacles seem to get in the way of me experiencing God's newness each day?

Driving Backwards

Don't be selfish; don't try to impress others. Be humble,
thinking of others as better than yourselves. Don't look out
only for your own interests, but take an interest in others, too.
~Philippians 2:3-4 (NLT)

Daniel laughed hysterically, "Mama, look at that truck! Why are we going backwards?" I followed his finger and looked at the semi-truck to our right. Either I slowed down, he sped up, or maybe we had perfect timing, but it seemed as if we were moving backwards.

From my vantage point as the driver, looking straight ahead, I was moving forward. From his spot in the backseat, the perspective was completely different; it honestly seemed like we were moving backwards. Our perspective depends on what seat we are sitting in.

Let's examine a road trip with my husband, as an example. As the driver, I am aware of the reasons why I do certain things, like, say, accidentally drive off the side of the road. Instead of swerving and possibly over-correcting, I might let my car stay in the grass a little bit longer. After several potholes, I slowly ease back onto the highway and resume the calm, peaceful ride. From my perspective, life is great, and an accident was averted. My husband, on the other hand, thinks I have lost control, begins stomping his imaginary brakes, grabs the "wait-a-minute" handle, and yells in my direction. Same scenario, but two totally different perspectives.

It's easy to view life through one set of lenses. I'm guilty. There are times when it seems easier to keep driving and gazing straight ahead, never looking outside my selfish little box. But if I would take the time to sit in the backseat and view the scenery from a different vantage point, I might realize that I am actually going backwards. I need to step back from time to time and look at things from someone else's perspective. What a narrow, selfish world I would live in if I only viewed life from the front seat.

Whose seat do I need to sit in this week and view life from their perspective?

Let's Live in the Deep-End

For you know that when your faith is tested, your endurance has a chance to grow. So let it grow, for when your endurance is fully developed, you will be perfect and complete, needing nothing.

~James 1:3-4 (NLT)

This summer my parents gave the boys swimming lessons every week. At the beginning, my oldest refused to get in the pool unless he was wearing his arm floats. He knew how to swim and did it well, but the idea of letting go of his security net scared him. My youngest, however, was the opposite. He was learning how to swim, and we had to make him put on his life vest and floats, otherwise, he dove in without thinking about the fact that he could possibly drown.

Their differences have made me examine my own life. Daniel laughs in the face of fear while Carter steps with hesitation. If Carter had not been forced to face his fear each week, he would still be in the shallow-end, wearing his floaties. He would have missed the confident resolve of conquering his fear and the resulting freedom of venturing into the deep-end.

Sometimes fear becomes the motivator for a sedentary life. Fear grows so large that we feel our feet taking root right where they stand. We forget that we are made for more. We forget the dream that is planted deep inside our hearts. We forget the passion that is hiding in our soul. We forget the deep-end even exists. And we forget that we already know how to swim. So, we stay stuck, not realizing the power that fear has over us.

But what if we force ourselves to face those fears? What if we take off our floaties and jump off that scary diving board? What if we stick our heads under the water and start swimming, even though we are scared? What if we stop living in nervous resistance and begin to solidly persevere? What if we embrace the confident resolve of conquering our fear and begin living in the true, unhindered freedom of the deep end? What if we learn to be completely free in Christ?

Am I living in the deep-end or am I still stuck wearing floaties?

Rip Up the Carpet

People who conceal their sins will not prosper, but if they confess and turn from them, they will receive mercy.
~Proverbs 28:13 (NLT)

The day we left for vacation, I decided to get rid of our flea problem by setting off a flea bomb in the house. We would be gone for five days and I could vacuum up any flea bodies before my toddler started crawling around on the floor. It was a good plan.

But then we came home and walked through the door. My white socks literally turned black with fleas. To say I came unglued was an understatement. By the time my husband got home from work the next day, his crazy, very pregnant wife had ripped up every piece of carpet in our house and thrown it into a giant pile on our front porch. The thought of my toddler and soon to be baby crawling around with all those fleas sent me into psycho-mama mode and I knew it was either the fleas or me.

And do you know what I found under that old carpet? A quarter inch layer of dirt filled with fleas and flea eggs! I was flabbergasted. All the treatments. All the vacuuming. All the chemicals. None of them did any good because I was only treating the top layer. It wasn't until I ripped that carpet off the floor's surface that I found the real culprit: a whole breeding ground for those disgusting little fleas.

I learned three things that day. I will never have carpet in my house again. Pregnant moms who are pushed to the crazy level can do some pretty irrational things. And sometimes we will never know the full extent of a problem until we are willing to do the hard work of ripping off the protectant layer.

What carpet in our lives have we been continually treating with topical solutions? Are we finding that no matter what we do, the fleas still keep coming back? Maybe it's time to do the extreme work of ripping up that protectant layer in our lives and start dealing with the fleas and eggs underneath. If we don't, those fleas will start taking over every area in our lives and it will soon be bigger than what those topical solutions can handle.

What sins am I hiding under the rug that need to be exposed?

Pockets of Joy

Blessed is the God and Father of our Lord Jesus Christ, who has blessed us with every spiritual blessing in the heavens in Christ.

~Ephesians 1:3 (CSB)

While I dressed Daniel in his overalls, I remembered the many hours I used to spend wearing my own pair of overalls. I loved filling up all the pockets with treasures of the day. Lady bugs, roly-polies, and rocks were just a few of the precious items I packed away in all the secret compartments. The zippered pockets were always my favorite because I didn't have to worry about losing any of my bugs or rocks. Oh, how I enjoyed storing up all those little treasures.

As I think about storing those sacred trinkets in my pockets, I can't help but think about the special treasures I have been storing up for myself lately. Every time someone says they are praying for us, I tuck it away in one of my pockets. When I get to spend time with special friends, I store it away in another pocket. Encouraging words get stashed to pull out on a later day. Laughs and giggles from my boys get pushed in close. But then there are those special moments where I feel like God sends just the right person, just the right song, or just the right scripture and those are the treasures that get zipped up so they won't fall out. Those are the moments that get me through the hard times.

Sometimes life can be all consuming and it feels like it won't let up. Other times the valleys outnumber the hills. But that's where these pockets of joy come in. When something makes us smile, tuck it away. When someone brings joy into our life, slip it away in another pocket. When we are blessed, loved, and valued, zip it up in that special pocket where it can't fall out. And when we need to be reminded of the good things, we simply reach in a pocket and pull that blessing out.

Even in hardship, there are pockets of joy. I'm thankful for a God who loves us enough to send us those blessings at just the right time.

What blessings do I need to pull out as a reminder of God's goodness, today?

Snake in the Chicken Pen

Give all your worries and cares to God, for he cares for you.
~1 Peter 5:7 (NLT)

There's a snake in the chicken pen!" my three-year-old screamed as he ran inside. My insides froze in terror. Thankfully, my husband had the wherewithal to think instead of freeze and grabbed the hoe. By the time I got the courage to step onto the front porch, David had already handled the situation and Mr. Snake was no more.

Carter came back inside shaking all over. The fear he felt was all too familiar. My husband looked at him sternly as we stood in the living room. "You still need to go feed those chickens, and check for eggs, Carter."

My little guy grabbed my hand, "Go with me, Mama?"

I wanted to say, *No, go ask your daddy because Mama is too yellow*, but I knew he needed Mama to be brave. Somehow I managed to pull on my big girl breeches, and we headed toward the chicken pen. My heart was racing, sweat was leaking from my forehead, but I knew Carter needed to see me be as brave as possible so he could be brave, too. I stepped in first, trying hard not to tremble, and I grabbed his hand. Together we looked around, carefully checked for snakes, and gathered the eggs. And yes, I might have done it really fast and on my tiptoes, just in case. But we did it, even though we were afraid.

Now hear me, I did not want to go into that chicken pen. But even more so, I did not want to pass my fear on to my son. So often my fear builds and cripples me. Even when I sense God is leading the charge and making a way, I still question, doubt, and feel scared. Afraid or not, I need to set the example and do it afraid.

I refuse to teach the next generation to live in fear, so I draw the line in the sand and do it afraid. The fear stops here.

What fears am I unintentionally passing onto my kids through my example?

Keep Your Feet on the Pedals

I prayed to the LORD, and he answered me. He freed me from all my fears.

~Psalm 34:4 (NLT)

My oldest has always struggled with balance, so that made learning to ride a bike a bit of a challenge. We did the training wheel thing, then we did the scooter thing, and now we are at the big kid stage where bikes don't come with training wheels. For his birthday we told him he had no choice—he had to learn to ride his new bike.

It was a disaster. He wore his boots. For all you first time parents out there, boots and bikes don't go together. His boots got stuck in the pedals, then they fell off the pedals. Then, his legs got scraped by the pedals, and it was an overall royal mess.

Trying our best to be good parents and continue with the motivation process, Daddy pushed and helped him balance on the dirt road. Carter cried. He yelled. Then his legs flailed out to the side. Finally, the bike fell over on our scared, anxious child. Our first lesson wasn't great.

He was afraid. Even with him wearing elbow and knee pads he was still so afraid. Afraid of falling. Afraid of embarrassment. And afraid of failing. We have been working on a strategy for the next time. We rehearse what being successful looks like and when he's ready, we will try again. And again. And again.

As my son battles his bicycle fear, I'm over here dealing with my own grown-up fears. Fear of stepping out into new things. Fear of what the school year will look like for my kids. Fear of not measuring up as a parent. Fear of rejection. Fear of judgment. And so many more.

But I can't let fear win. Neither can you. We need to have our own defensive strategies in place, talk through the fears, and rehearse our victorious move. Fear cannot win or flailing legs overcome with uncontrollable chaos will cause us to crash right into the ditch.

So, we hop on our bikes, fix our eyes on Jesus, and trust Him with the rest.

Is God asking me to step out in any areas that seem a little scary?

Spiderboy

You will keep in perfect peace those whose minds are stead-
fast, because they trust in you.

~Isaiah 26:3 (NIV)

My youngest has reached the age of independence. He thinks
he can get himself clean enough in the shower and doesn't want
help. The other night he was stubbornly insistent, so I said, "Fine.
You go take a shower all alone." Mr. Bigshot strutted toward the
bathroom, grinning the whole way. He could do it all by himself.

Next thing I knew, I heard a blood curdling scream. I rounded
the corner, thinking he had hurt himself. When I pulled back the
curtain, he looked like Spider-Man up in the back corner of the
bathtub. The shower head was shooting ice cold water and he was
shivering. "You can do it all by yourself, huh?"

Smiling, but still frozen on the edge of the tub, he sweetly
pleaded, "I can wash me. But can you fix the water? It's
fuh-fuh-freeeeezinggg!"

I snickered as I rescued Mr. Bigshot.

As my overzealous five-year-old discovered, what we expect
doesn't always happen. He expected the water to automatically
be the right temperature, but instead he was shocked because he
didn't mix the hot water with the cold.

His little lesson in expectations resonated with me this week. I
made some big decisions and let some things go that have been
a part of my life for a decade. New directions and new doors are
opening, and I need to be available to say yes when the opportunities present themselves. But those opportunities aren't here yet.

I'm letting go in faith. And honestly, when I let go, I thought I would automatically know the next step. But I don't.

Trusting in my expectations let me down. I second guessed myself all week as a result of leaning on my expectations instead of trusting God. What we expect doesn't always happen. And it sure doesn't happen in our timing. I need to learn to do it because it's the right thing to do and will honor God, not because of expectations. That's a hard one.

Am I hoping in my own expectations or trusting in God's divine hand?

God, You Are Just So Good

*The LORD is good to everyone. He showers compassion on
all his creation.*

~Psalm 145:9 (NLT)

Confession. Bedtime prayers with my kids have never been a
thing. I hug and tuck them in but remembering to pray has always
slipped my mind. After many months of self-imposed mom guilt, I
decided to create our own special prayer time on the way to school
in the mornings.

Most days, after my oldest reads a short devotion, one of my
boys will say a prayer. It's usually something like this: "Thank you,
God, for letting Dada have a good day. And Frank (our dog). And
Bob and Dan (horses we gave away four years ago). And Francis
(our Compassion child). And Mama. And thank you for letting
everyone in the whole wide world have a good day. In Jesus name.
Amen." There are days of variation that may include Scruffy (our
cat), Cedrick (the name for every squirrel who decides to run in
front of our car), or a spelling test they have that day.

One particular Tuesday morning, however, it was my five-year-
old's turn to pray. He got very still, folded his hands, and a giant
smile spread across his face, "God," he paused, and the smile grew
bigger. "You are just SOOOO good."

I couldn't tell you what the rest of the prayer was that morning
because tears slid down my cheeks and a smile spread across my
face. As I replayed my five-year-old's words in my head, I was able
to see snapshots of God's goodness spread all over my life, even
though it's been one tough year.

As I closed my eyes at the end of the day, a smile completed my face as a new prayer completed my day. "God, you are just SOOOO good." And I laid there counting my blessings as if they were sheep until I fell asleep.

Do I truly believe that God is good? What blessings do I need to start counting every day?

Mama, Do You Need Some Attention?

Dear friends, let us continue to love one another, for love comes from God. Anyone who loves is a child of God and knows God.

~1 John 4:7 (NLT)

Mama, do you need some attention?" Daniel asked. I wiped the tears from my cheeks and pulled him into my lap.

"I sure do. What kind of attention do you think I need?"

"Hmm," I could see the wheels turning as I regained my composure. "Let's sing," he said. After a few minutes of the two of us belting out music at the top of our lungs, a big smile spread across my face. My sweet little boy had no idea how much joy he brought to my hurting heart.

"Thank you, sweet boy. Mama really did need some attention. But I am better now."

Daniel leaned in, wrapped his arms around my neck, and gave me the biggest hug he could muster. "Love you, Mama," and then he jumped down and went back to playing.

My heart was so heavy that particular day as my husband was in the middle of cancer treatments. Daniel didn't know. But God did. And He sent that silly, loud, huggy, little boy to me at just the right moment.

And He wants us to do that for others. That person who keeps running through our brains—we need to stop and call them. That text that we keep meaning to send—we need to send it. That card we intended to mail to an old friend—we need to mail it. We all need a little bit of attention sometimes and God wants to use each of us in the lives of others to show His love. Let's be obedient.

Am I following through with the people God needs me to show attention toward?

They are God's First

And we know that God causes everything to work together for the good of those who love God and are called according to his purpose for them.

~Romans 8:28 (NLT)

Daniel needs to be admitted to the hospital today," the doctor instructed.

I called David to pack some overnight bags, scheduled Carter to stay with Grandma, and within an hour, we were headed to Tallahassee. At five months old, our little guy only weighed twelve and a half pounds. He always had trouble with congestion, and even a small sniffle meant days of labored breathing. When our doctor said RSV and sent us to the hospital, we became scared.

Seeing my tiny boy hooked up to oxygen and all the wires is a picture I will never forget. For three days he fought fever, congestion, and struggled to keep his air flow stable. Sleep was not something that happened much for me during that hospital stay. I remember standing over him as he fitfully slept. I pleaded with God through tears; begged Him to heal our little boy. There was desperation in my cries. God's intervention was the only way we would get to take our little boy home with us and all I knew to do was place Daniel in His hands.

Daniel was entrusted into our care at birth by our Almighty God. Why He ever chose us, I may never know, but He did. That night, as I stood over Daniel in tears, I had to accept an even deeper reality—he is not mine to keep, only on loan, and if God chose to take him, I had to let him go. I wrestled all night with leaving my baby in God's hands and trusting that His plan was way better than mine.

As the sun came up, I finally let go. And day three was the day Daniel made a huge turn around. By that evening, his breathing was better, and we were on our way home. But the lesson I learned in that hospital room is one that I remind myself of often: my boys are God's first. I have the privilege of loving them here on earth as long as God allows, and part of loving them is trusting that God knows best in all situations. My prayer continues to be that I love them deep, wide, and well every day there is breath in my lungs.

Do I trust you totally with my children, God?

Extra Underwear

*Preach the word of God. Be prepared, whether the time
is favorable or not. Patiently correct, rebuke, and encourage
your people with good teaching.*

~2 Timothy 4:2 (NLT)

Mama, I need you to do something for me for the rest of my life,"
Daniel told me one morning.

"And what would that be?"

"Will you pick out my clothes and hang them up for me every
morning forever? I get too distracted."

I was intrigued by his self-awareness. "Maybe not the rest of
your life, but how about until you finish kindergarten?"

"Deal," he said and stuck his hand out. I shook it and smiled.

Fast forward a few months.

"Mama," Daniel rounded the corner laughing hysterically, "guess
what I did." He lifted up his shirt and showed me. "I put on two
pairs of underwear this morning. Look." Sure enough, an orange
pair and a blue pair. How did he manage to do that when I laid
out his clothes every day?

"Didn't you go to the bathroom today? How did you not notice
the fact that you had on two pairs of underwear?"

"I don't know. But I know now," and with that he went about his
afternoon without another thought.

As usual, I began thinking. Do I take in just enough of God's
Word to have one layer of underwear, or am I doubling up and getting
that extra dose? Am I overly prepared in my walk with Christ to the
point that it's second nature and I don't realize I've got two pairs on?

In season and out of season, day or night, home or work—we must be prepared and ready to tell of all that God has done in our lives. We need to double up and be ready.

Am I spending time with God every day so I can be ready at all times to share?

"Code One, Register Three"

*They do not fear bad news; they confidently trust the L*ORD *to care for them.*

~Psalm 112:7 (NLT)

Excuse me, ma'am," the lady leaned in close to the cashier. "As I was leaving, I noticed a little mouse outside the sliding doors. He is trying to come inside your lobby. I just wanted you to know." I was at the checkout counter with my kids. We turned our gaze just in time to see the mouse sitting in the lobby between two shelving units.

The cashier thanked the woman and with panic in her eyes picked up the phone, "Code one, register three. Code one, register three." As soon as she hung up, another associate quickly appeared by her side, whispering and pointing. "You see him? He's right there. I'm going to ring this lady up. But we gotta get that thing out of here."

"Daniel. Carter. Do you guys want to catch a mouse?" I asked the boys loud enough for the cashier to hear.

"Yeah! We'll get him!" They took off for the lobby as I focused back on the cashier who looked relieved.

"So, I have a question for you. I noticed you called code one for the mouse. Do you guys really have a code for critters?"

The cashier nervously laughed. "No girl, we don't. But I think we need one now!"

About that time the boys ran back over giving all the details of the mouse hunt.

"I had my hands on him and Carter almost kicked him, but then he ran back out the door. We think."

"We hope," said the cashier. "I don't do rats. No way. Thanks, boys."

As I gathered my items and listened to the rat story recapped by my sons, I thought about how unprepared the staff was for a mouse. The little fellow blindsided them; they had no idea what to do.

Life tends to the do the same thing. We are living our lives in a normal way when suddenly a mouse enters our lobby. Confusion, fear, and concern take over. All we can think to do is call code one, hoping someone will show up who knows how to handle it better than we do.

When the unexpected comes, let God be our Code One. He will come to our rescue and handle every situation way better than we ever will. Even a mouse in the lobby.

Am I trusting God with the unexpected situations that come my way or do I try to handle them alone?

I Don't Want to be a City Boy

*But Jesus told him, "Anyone who puts a hand to the plow
and then looks back is not fit for the Kingdom of God."*
~Luke 9:62 (NLT)

Mama," Daniel began, "I am so glad I don't have to live in the city."

Interested in his reasoning, I followed up. "Well, why would you say that? There is nothing wrong with living in the city. I grew up in town, road bikes, played with friends, and had a really good time."

He thought for a minute. "Well I guess it's not bad for everyone. It's just not for me."

"Why not?"

"See, in the country I get to play outside and ride my go-cart. You can't do that in town."

"That's true. Go-carts are not welcome in town—"

"But really the biggest and onliest reason is that I can't go to the bathroom in the yard if I lived in town."

His matter of fact reply and voice inflection had me laughing. It seemed like such a silly reason. Of all the better arguments he could have come up with, it all came down to the convenience of going to the bathroom in the front yard. Spoken like a true country boy.

But what about us? What kinds of crazy excuses and reasons do we come up with for staying where we are when God starts tugging at our hearts and leading us toward surrender? How many silly ideas or notions do we throw at God when all He wants is our yes?

"God, I really like this ministry because I know what to do. It's easy. It's comfortable. It's familiar. It's safe." Or "God, I'm not in the best shape for that mission trip. And you know how I am about germs. And airports. It's just not for me." Or "Fostering children isn't my thing. All those bad behaviors are too much for me to deal with. Give me my own kids for now and their friends on the weekends. I can handle that."

Just like my son, our reasoning isn't up to par. God simply wants our yes, not our excuses. Even if using the bathroom off the front porch is a wonderful convenience, maybe God has something else in store for us.

Am I really listening to you, God, or have I already made up my mind before I give your direction a second glance?

Too Much Gatorade

In any case, we should live up to whatever truth we have attained.

~Philippians 3:16 (CSB)

Listen, little boy. Stop pestering me about wanting my drink. You are big enough to get your own Gatorade. Go into the kitchen, use your stool, get a cup, fill it with water, and put the Gatorade mix into your cup. You don't need Mama to stand over you." Famous last words.

Daniel took off up the steps and ran into the house to live in this new found freedom. After a few minutes, he came down the steps with a kid's sized plastic cup. "Boy this Gatorade is sure sugary," he said as he loudly slurped the juice from his cup. He smiled and his tongue was bright orange, as were his teeth.

"What makes it sugary, Daniel? How many scoops did you put in there?"

"I decided to stop at four. That seemed like enough."

"Four whole scoops?" He nodded back at me. "Daniel, four scoops is enough to make a whole gallon. Like the size of a milk jug. Not for a little boy to mix in that tiny cup! No wonder it seems so sugary!"

"Ohhhh. That might be why," he said as he dumped the orange stream of powdery residue down his chin on the last slurp.

In his defense, I assumed he had watched me make Gatorade. I assumed he knew he was supposed to stir the powder once he added it to the water in his cup. I assumed he knew a quarter of a scoop was all he needed. But all my assumptions were wrong.

As Christians, we do the same thing. We assume that others

should be at a certain Christian maturity level or have a particular theological background. We assume that marriage is regarded highly by all or that every parent disciplines and protects their kids the same as we do. But the bad thing about assumptions is that most of the time, we are dead wrong. We are all at a different place in this Christian walk thing and we can't assume. Each of us must make the effort to teach and disciple other believers. Never should we expect that someone has reached a certain level of understanding simply because of their age or status. We can only live up to the truth to which we have attained.

In my assumptions of others, do I have any unrealistic expectations that need to be addressed?

Thomas the Train Baby

Oh Israel, the one who formed you says, "Do not be afraid, for I have ransomed you. I have called you by name; you are mine."

~Isaiah 43:1 (NLT)

Carter, we have some exciting news. The baby growing inside of Mama's belly is going to be a little boy, like you."

"A brudder?" He asked excitedly. "A little brudder?"

I nodded and smiled. "And we want you to help us name him. So, think about it a few days." Carter was a very deliberate child and I knew he needed some time to think about it.

"I already know, Mama," he reached out and put his hands on my belly, "Thomas the Train Baby. We can call him Train Baby."

He was completely serious, so I maintained my composure. "Well, Thomas is a good name to consider, but we already have a Thomas as a relative. Don't you have any other names you want to call him?"

"Nope. He is Thomas the Train Baby." With that statement he walked off and left me standing there wondering what in the world I was thinking letting a four-year-old name his new baby brother.

The next morning Carter came barreling into the living room, "I know now. Not Thomas the Train Baby. Daniel Tiger."

I liked the idea of Daniel, but not the Tiger part. "What if we named him just Daniel and let Daddy come up with his middle name?"

Carter thought hard for a few minutes, "Okay. Deal."

Names can be tricky sometimes. We have the name we are given at birth, but we also have other names. There are the names others have called us. The names we have associated with ourselves in the deep recesses of our minds. The names we wish we were known as. And the names we wish weren't true.

But God knows our name and He whispers it deep in our soul. He reminds us, "You are mine." We are not the untrue names others have called us. We are not the negative words we label ourselves with. We are not called by the things we have done. We are known, by name, through the grace-filled eyes of Christ. He is our true identity.

Do I cling to the names that I associate with myself, or do I find my true identity in Christ and what He says of me?

Daniel Rides Shotgun

Two people are better off than one, for they can help each
other succeed. If one person falls, the other person can reach
out and help, but someone who falls alone is in real trouble.
~Ecclesiastes 4:9-10 (NLT)

Okay, boys. Your final present," I handed them the boxes and
watched paper fly all over the place.

"What are these for?"They held the helmets in their hands with
a puzzled expression.

"Carter, Daddy promised he would have the go-cart fixed and
ready on your sixth birthday and today is the day." Carter raced
out the door.

"Wait for me!" Little two-year-old Daniel yelled as he hurried
behind his big brother.

My husband worked for months getting this second-hand buggy
running for Carter's birthday, and now the moment was here. The
governor was set on the gas pedal, the seat belts were set for little
people, and their helmets secured and fastened. We had been teaching Carter for several years how to drive different farm buggies
while he was in our laps, but now was the moment of truth.

They hopped in, and Carter took off around field out front. I had
no idea how Daniel would like it and hoped he didn't come back
crying. As they descended the hill toward us, Daniel had a huge
smile on his face. His arm was propped on the side bar like a grown
man in a truck window—they were having the time of their life.

"Daniel, what did you think about the ride with Carter?" I asked
as they parked.

"It fast. It fun. Do again!" he said as he jumped in the air.

It's been four years and these two boys still love to ride together. They tell me it's always the most fun when they are both riding together. Life's the same way. It's always more fun having someone in the passenger seat. The twists and turns might be a little scary all alone, but when there is someone to share those moments with, they don't look all that scary.

God designed us to be in relationship with other people. How does this area look in your life? Do you think you are better off alone? Or are you enjoying the benefits of having a friend who rides shotgun? Two are always better than one.

Am I actively engaging and participating in relationships with others, or have I pulled away in isolation?

Baby Godzilla

As a dog returns to its vomit so a fool repeats his foolishness.
~Proverbs 26:11 (NLT)

When Daniel was a new toddler, we affectionately referred to him as Baby Godzilla. He walked on his first birthday, and he ran the very next day. His arms were in the air, mouth wide-open, and he made this "monsterish" growling noise as he kicked, stomped, and destroyed anything that got in his way. He picked up trucks, trains, Transformers, and tractors, and threw them with all his might at whoever or whatever was in his path. Everything was tasted or licked, including boots, toes, cats, and glasses. He was such a busy, disgusting, destructive child during those few months and boy, did he make his older brother mad.

"Carter, pick up your toys. Daniel will break them." I felt like I was a broken record repeating this phrase again and again. And sure enough, no sooner had the words left my lips than Daniel grabbed one of his toys and threw it across the room.

One particular day, Carter sat on the floor building a new creation with blocks. His tower was almost as tall as he was when Baby Godzilla rounded the corner. "No, Daniel. These are my blocks. Don't touch them," Carter commanded.

Daniel grinned. I ran interference and instructed him not to mess with Carter's blocks. For a while he listened. He played with the dog. Then drove the trains on the floor. Carter lost interest in his towers and set up his cars on the couch.

"Carter, if you want those towers to survive, you need to move them out of Daniel's reach. You know Baby Godzilla will tear them down."

"I will get them later," Carter replied.

And then the holy terror himself realized the towers were without protection. Even though he knew he wasn't supposed to, that destructive inclination rose to the top. Like a scene from a monster movie, Daniel threw his arms in the air, growled, and trampled the towers to smithereens.

We do the same thing. Even though we know we shouldn't do it and it's the wrong thing, we do it anyway. We allow destructive attitudes, habits, and behaviors to rise to the top, and just like Daniel, we throw those arms in the air, we make that defiant growl, and do it anyway.

What destructive attitudes, habits, or behaviors do I have unchecked in my life that need to be surrendered to Jesus?

He Licks Everything

Taste and see that the LORD is good. Oh, the joys of those who take refuge in him!

~Psalm 34:8 (NLT)

Seriously, stop! Do you know where my boot has been? Don't lick my boot." Daniel ran off giggling as my husband shooed him away.

Later that day, we were sitting beside the firepit, playing with toy trucks, and enjoying the evening. "Daniel, stop. That cat has so many yucky germs on her. Don't lick the cat," I instructed.

Five minutes later, "Daniel, come on, really? Everything does not need your tongue on it. Stop licking your brother."

All week, everywhere we went, Daniel was constantly licking things. Doorknobs, people, pets, glasses, furniture, toys, cars, and even the floor. No matter what we told him or showed him about germs, he kept on tasting everything.

Finally, we sat down for supper one night, and he was too distracted to eat. "Daniel," I began, "all week long, you have been putting your tongue where it doesn't belong and now, I'm telling you to use it, and you won't even pay attention long enough to lick your food." He giggled, but got the point, and began eating his supper.

It got me thinking, though. How often am I more interested in tasting the things of this world than I am for sampling the things of God? I get wrapped up in a television series, the local gossip, or wasting time on social media and I neglect time with God in the Word, through prayer, and in song.

If I am truly going to taste and see that the Lord is good, I must make sure that my hunger is for Him and not for the world. Just like Daniel, licking the things of this world is going to make me sick. I need to seek after and taste the things of the Lord in all areas of my life.

What areas of this world are you hungering after and tasting that need to be traded out for the goodness of the Lord?

Rule #6
Don't Attack Mama with the Drone

The LORD doesn't see things the way you see them. People judge by outward appearance, but the LORD looks at the heart.
~1 Samuel 16:7b (NLT)

Carter has always been my rule follower. When he was in kindergarten, he came home the first week of school and taught me all the rules of the classroom, complete with detailed motions. "Rule number one: Listen when the teacher is talking. Rule number two: Follow directions quickly. Rule number three: Raise your hand and wait for permission to speak or leave your seat. Rule number four: Respect others, respect yourself, respect your school. Rule number five: Be safe, be kind, be honest."

When he was rambunctious, a simple reference to his new kindergarten rules was all he needed to quickly corrected any misbehavior. He adored his new kindergarten teacher and loved the fact that he was such a good rule follower.

One afternoon, I was relaxing outside in the hammock while my husband was playing with his new drone. David buzzed me a few times, which Carter found hilarious. It was funny the first few times, but then the drone got too close and nicked my arm. My pleasant afternoon in the hammock quickly turned sour. I tried to move out of the war path, but of course, I got stuck in the hammock, which made me an easy target for more attacks.

When I finally got up, I walked over to Carter and said, "Okay, I want you to say all those rules you're always reciting." He looked at me with a puzzled expression, but soon rattled off all five. "Okay,

I'm adding another rule. Rule number six: Don't attack Mama with a drone." David and Carter both belly laughed as Carter made up the motions for rule number six.

Rules are an important part of life, even silly ones about drones. They keep us safe and help maintain order. But rules can also hold us captive. Carter was obsessed with the rules and he wanted to follow them even when he was at home. Fearfully he obeyed, worried that a minor misstep would cause major failure.

As Christians, it can be tempting to simply follow the rules, check off all the boxes, but miss out on the deeper pieces of relationship with Jesus. God looks at our hearts, and if we are only going through the motions, then all our effort and work is for nothing. We must learn the rules, but live by the Spirit.

Am I a rule follower out of habit, or am I truly seeking a deeper relationship with the Lord?

Walking Wounded

He heals the brokenhearted and bandages their wounds.
~Psalm 147:3 (NLT)

Mama, what does lame mean? Dada said the rocky horse went lame."

"When a real horse or animal is lame, it means that animal cannot walk anymore; something is wrong with their legs."

Daniel thought for a minute. "But the rocky horse doesn't have legs. How did it go lame?"

I snickered, "Dada was making a joke. People say their horse is lame when it can't go anymore. The rocky horse can't go anymore because the rope is broken."

As the lightbulb came on for Daniel, it also came on for me. We walk around wounded all the time. Emotionally lame. Beaten up by circumstances, abuse, neglect, and fear. Spiritually limping. Harboring questions and doubts about God's love, faithfulness, goodness, and fairness. Mentally weak. Overwhelmed by responsibilities, decisions, and obligations. Physically exhausted. Bodies bent under the weight of the spiritual, mental, and emotional overload along with any other physical ailments we might already have.

But we keep trying to walk even though we are wounded. And as we go, we bleed our brokenness on others. But we never stop. And we never give our wound a name. We never call it bitterness. Or unforgiveness. We never call it insecurity. Or fear. We just keep walking while the wound gets larger under the protective layers we place on top.

We create protective boundaries. Isolate. And we go through the motions.

Lame. Limping. Weak. Exhausted. Wounded.

Then what happens? "The rocky horse can't go anymore because it's broken." Eventually we lose ourselves. Our passions. Our love. Our belief. Our faith. Our relationships. Our hope.

Am I laying on the ground, lame like my son's rocky horse, simply medicating the problem or am I naming it and dealing with at the foot of the cross?

Halloween is Over Already!

But I focus on this one thing: Forgetting the past and looking forward to what lies ahead, I press on to reach the end of the race and receive the heavenly prize for which God, through Christ Jesus, is calling us.

~Philippians 3:13b-14 (NLT)

Halloween is over already!" Daniel cried from the backseat. Elephant tears ran down his cheeks as he boohooed all the way home. "No more costumes. No more candy. No more running around with friends."

Halloween is a big deal to little kids. My sons have planned their costume seventeen times in the past year, and they already told me their ideas for next Halloween.

"Well, you know," I tried to console him, "you can wear your costume anytime you want to now that Halloween is over. You can even sleep in it."

Another burst of emotion followed by more tears. "It's not the same! I never wanted it to end. I miss Halloween." At this point his words were jumbled with overwhelming kid-sadness and there was nothing left to do but let him cry it out.

His deep expression of emotion made me think about my own season of expectation. I have been working all year to get prepared for the conference I attended two weeks ago. The anticipation was agonizing at times as the excitement welled up inside. And just like that, it was over, and I was flung back into the real world of cancer treatments, organizing two big outreach events, and the general hustle and bustle of life with two young kids. I wanted it to last longer. I wanted time to let the new ideas, material, and relationships marinate deep inside my soul. I wanted the inspiration to permeate every orifice on my body and fill me so full that I was oozing with life and encouragement.

Like my son realized, all wonderful things come to an end and we can't live in the moments of the past; we have to move ahead because time doesn't stand still. But, I can take my own advice to my son and "wear my costume anytime I want". I can continue to pursue my dreams. I can continue to live. And I can continue trying to honor God through it all, no matter what may come my way. It may not be the same as Halloween, but I can carry sparks of excitement with me as I intentionally wear my costume any time I want.

Am I wishing away my future by holding onto the good things from the past or am I embracing the future as I actively pursue Christ?

Pick Up Those Nails

We will not hide these truths from our children; we will
tell the next generation about the glorious deeds of the LORD,
about his power and his mighty wonders.

~Psalm 78:4 (NLT)

My sons and I were out for a walk one afternoon, enjoying the cool breeze and the busy wildlife. We live on the family farm, but we also have a section of land that we lease to a company to dig fill dirt. Heavy equipment, dump trucks, and many personal vehicles drive through our property daily, so I am constantly looking for nails, glass, or pieces of metal that could leave someone stranded because of a busted tire.

This particular day, I had already collected several nails, a piece of wire, a hunk of metal, and a large bolt as we were walking. "Mama," Daniel asked, "why are you picking up all that junk and putting it in your pockets?"

"I want to make sure the way is safe for the trucks that are coming down this road later. If I leave this nail in the road, it might get in someone's tire, and then they won't be able to drive their vehicle until they can fix the tire," I replied.

"Yeah," Carter jumped in, "like our go-cart could get a flat tire from a nail and we have to walk home."

Suddenly the light came on with my youngest and he started picking up sharp broken objects, too. By the time we finished our walk, we had quite the collection. "I hope you see what we did here, guys. We always want to make it easier on the people coming behind us. If we can make a trail through the woods, or build a bridge over a creek, or simply pick up nails in the road, we can make this stretch of road better for someone else." The boys nodded that they understood.

As parents we have the great privilege of picking up our own nails so our children who come behind us don't step on them and get wounded. We need to learn to pick up our fears, past hurts, and jaded views so our children don't latch onto them. We also have to be careful not to leave our junk scattered, like a destructive, marked trail wherever we go. Our nails can be sharp. Our nails can be pointed. Our nails can be deadly. But we want the path to be clear for the next generation, no matter what it takes.

God, what nails am I carelessly leaving along the path behind me?

Fat and Fluffy

May the words of my mouth and the meditation of my
heart be pleasing to you, O LORD, my rock and my redeemer.
~Psalm 19:14 (NLT)

Mama!" Daniel yelled loudly across the restaurant as he stood in the booth and pointed. "Look at that lady with the crazy hair. She's fat."

Horrified, I grabbed his hand and put him back in the sitting position. Silently I mouthed, "I'm sorry," to the lady across the room who was now staring at me. "Daniel, we don't say things like that about people. Those kinds of words will hurt their feelings."

"But Mama, her hair is crazy. And she's fat," Daniel replied with a confused expression on his face.

"All truths don't have to be expressed and pointed out. If someone is overweight, they already know. They don't need a four-year-old kid pointing it out in public. And just because you think her hair is crazy doesn't mean that she thinks it is. Be careful with your words. They can hurt people." I could tell he was thinking. "And by the way, the word fat is no longer allowed. If you feel the need to describe someone who is overweight, you need to use the word fluffy."

Daniel sat quietly eating his pizza, obviously still thinking. A grin spread across his face. "Well, Mama, I think you're fluffy."

I smiled, "Alright Mr. Smarty Pants. You better be glad I love you." I hugged him and we laughed.

Then I thought about the power of our words. The phrases, nicknames, taunts, and chants of childhood still stick with me and many other people too. Deep pain, hurt, and insecurity can be attached to words that were carelessly tossed around.

As parents, we need to not only teach our kids the right words, but also remember our words become the inner dialogue that is being played in the heads of our children. Are we building them up or tearing them down?

God, am I influencing the mindset and emotional health of my children for the better with my words?

Francis the Monkey

*"I, yes I, am the one who comforts you. So why are you afraid
of mere humans, who wither like the grass and disappear?*
~Isaiah 51:12 (NLT)

Look, Mama." I stopped what I was doing and looked at my two-
year-old son. "Me. Francis. Match." Francis the monkey, Carter's
favorite stuffed animal was dressed in an orange shirt, blue shorts,
hat, and shoes, just like Carter was wearing.

"Well, hi, Francis," I replied, "and just where are you two going
this morning?"

Carter's dimples deepened with his grin. "Watch Thomas," he
replied as he tucked Francis under his arm. And off he ran back
into the living room.

Francis and Carter have been inseparable for years. Sleepovers
with the grandmas, road trips, doctor visits, and morning snuggles
in the recliner all include Francis the monkey. There's something
comforting about a stuffed animal, especially one that has been a
part of a child's world since they were small. I still have my stuffed
monkey, Munchy-Coo, from when I was a kid. I carried him everywhere when I was younger.

Carter is now ten and his friends are getting too old for stuffed
animals. "Mama, do I have to stop sleeping with Francis?" Tears
filled his eyes. "I don't want to, but my friends said that stuffed
animals are for babies."

"Oh, Carter," I invited him to sit in my lap. I wrapped my arms
around him and Francis. "Don't tell anyone, but I slept with my
teddy bear, Fuzzy, until after I got married. You know the white,

fuzzy bear you and Daniel have now, he used to be one of my stuffed animals." Carter smiled. "And don't you listen to those boys at school. If you want to sleep with Francis until you are a grown up, you do it. There's nothing wrong with it."

He gave me a big hug, "Thanks, Mama."

As I recall this moment, I'm grateful to God for being my comfort. When the nights are long and the days are hard, He is always there. When I'm afraid and doubting, He assures me and directs my steps. When I'm lonely and feel forsaken, He swoops in and reminds me whose I am.

God, am I depending on you and allowing you to comfort me as I go about this everyday life, or have I shamefully tucked you aside thinking I can do it alone?

Balancing on Scooters

The Lord directs the steps of the godly, He delights in every detail of their lives.

~Psalm 37:23 (NLT)

We tried the whole bike thing with Carter. Training wheels worked great on a small bicycle, but on a grown-up sized bike they looked out of place. Since his struggles with the bike appeared to be balance related, we bought the boys scooters for Christmas. The slab for our house was recently poured, so it would be a great place for the boys to practice riding and work on their balance.

I don't know how many miles they put on those scooters over the Christmas holiday. Every waking moment was spent riding in circles, chasing each other on those scooters.

Then they asked if we could take the scooters on the bike trail across town. We loaded helmets, scooters, water, and kids and made our way to the trail. Balancing on the trail was trickier than our concrete slab at home. Cracks in the asphalt from roots growing underneath made humps and hills in unpredictable places. Sticks, pinecones, and sand washed down from the dirt road. Some places were slick with mud and there were even occasional piles of animal dung that needed to be avoided.

About a mile away from the truck, Carter hit a big crack way too hard causing him and the scooter to fall on the asphalt. A scraped knee, a bunch of blood, and a bruised ego made the trip back to the truck seem like forever. There was crying, wailing, and plenty of drama associated with this knee-scraping event.

As I think back to that moment, I can see the problem. He wasn't used to the new terrain, and he didn't anticipate so many obstacles since he had nothing but smooth concrete at the house. But his experience is not unlike the journey we are on. We can't always anticipate the cracks and debris in the road. We aren't always sure where the slick mud will show up or when to step wide to avoid a large pile of poo.

Just like those scooters on rough terrain, navigating life can be quite the balancing act. I'm grateful God promises to be with us and guide our every step; that He already knows what lies ahead before we ever make it there.

God, am I trusting you to help me navigate the rough terrain or am I bruised up from the fall and resisting your help?

Hickory Nuts in Our Pipes

And now, dear brothers and sisters, one final thing. Fix your thoughts on what is true, and honorable, and right, and pure, and lovely, and admirable. Think about things that are excellent and worthy of praise.

~Philippians 4:8 (NLT)

Hello in there!" Daniel's voice echoed in the long pipe that was laying in the yard. There were over a dozen pieces of pipe scattered around as we prepared for the next stage of our house build. Soon these pipes would all be buried with a few small pieces sticking out of the ground for sink and toilet drains.

Daniel loved playing with the pipes. When we finished the concrete slab, he intentionally investigated each pipe. Curiously, he shined his flashlight into the openings and stuck his tiny hands as far as he could into each pipe.

Soon he found sticks and long pieces of metal that he stuck into the pipes to see how far they would go before he had to pull them out. At this point we stepped in, "Daniel, please don't stick things into the pipes. They might break off and get stuck in there. We need them clear and open so our drain will work properly. Why don't you play with the cat awhile? Maybe she will chase one of your sticks or maybe even some string."

The next thing I know, Daniel had gathered up a bucket full of hickory nuts and was rolling them across the slab for the cat to chase. The two of them had everyone laughing. Assuming he was sufficiently distracted, I went around the front to work on another project. Ten minutes later, I rounded the corner to see my son stuffing one of the drains with hickory nuts. After living in a home with drainage problems, I could see all our hard work and effort literally going down the drain.

Immediately, Daniel and I had a long talk and decided hickory nuts would be better for throwing in the yard or to the cat. But as I think back to that day, I can't help but wonder what wrong stuff we are putting in our pipes. Just like Daniel was stuffing those pipes full of nuts, what junk am I shoving into my brain and heart that will eventually clog up all my spiritual piping?

Am I paying attention to the hickory nuts that I'm putting into my mind and heart?

Baby in the Mirror

For if you listen to the word and don't obey, it is like glancing at your face in a mirror. You see yourself, walk away, and forget what you look like. But if you look carefully into the perfect law that sets you free, and if you do what it says and don't forget what you heard, then God will bless you for doing it.

~James 1:23-25 (NLT)

W ho's that baby?" Daniel slowly peeked around the corner and looked at the baby in the mirror. His toothless grin grew from ear to ear followed by a giggle. "I see him. Who's that baby?" We peeked and giggled for a half hour. He pushed the mirrored glass, trying to reach the baby on the other side.

For weeks after that day, he wanted to stand on the counter and stare at the baby in the mirror. "Beh beh," he'd say as he patted the reflection of himself. "Chiss," he said as he scooted over where he could see the whole baby in the mirror. He leaned in and gave the baby a kiss, looked back at me, and clapped. "Chiss. Beh beh."

"Yes, you did kiss the baby. That was sweet," I replied as I set him back on the floor. He toddled to the living room and on the television was a commercial.

"Beh beh," he pointed excitedly at the television.

"That's right. Baby. Good job."

Just like Daniel was able to recognize the baby in the mirror, he also recognized a baby in the living room. It wasn't just a one time deal, he recognized the "beh beh" wherever he went. The same should be true for us. We shouldn't just look into the mirror of God's Word once a week on Sundays and then neglect reading the rest of the week. That would be like not recognizing ourselves in the mirror each time we look.

Instead, we should take heed and hear what God says, doing everything in our power to follow him in our everyday lives. Just like Daniel recognized the baby, we should recognize God's direction in our lives and actively acknowledge it.

Have I forgotten what my life should look like if I'm truly striving to be like Christ?

I Want a Mohawk

Such people claim they know God, but they deny him by the way they live.

~Titus 1:16a (NLT)

I want a mohawk," Daniel announced one evening during summer break.

"Okay, let's get the clippers," and we made his dream a reality. "Now listen, if you don't like it, you have to give it at least 24 hours before we cut it off. Deal?"

"Deal," he replied.

The summer before, the mohawk lasted 12 hours because he didn't like the texture of the hair gel, so unless this was a new child sitting in front of me, I knew he wouldn't last long.

"Let's spike it before bed and see what it looks like," I told him. He excitedly ran into the master bathroom and let me spike it with hair product. I lifted him up to see himself in the mirror and his face lit up.

"I love it!" He ran to the other end of the house and called for his brother. "Carter, Carter. Look at my mohawk. I look like a rockstar dude."

The next morning, I called Daniel into my bedroom. "Are you ready for me to stand your hair up?"

"Nope."

"I thought you wanted a mohawk," I replied.

"I do, but I don't want it spiked."

"Do you want me to cut it off tonight?

"Nope," he said. "I like it flat."

Needless to say, Daniel now has a mohawk, but it doesn't stand up. It's like calling myself a Christian but not standing for Christ. I might go to church, socialize in Christian circles, and align myself with politicians who share similar values as mine, but if I don't share my faith or allow Jesus to shine through my life, what good is a declaration? I am like Daniel's mohawk that doesn't stand up.

Am I only declaring my Christianity with my words or am I taking a stand and living it out in my daily life?

Just Pull It Out

Throw off your old sinful nature and your former way of life, which is corrupted by lust and deception. Instead, let the Spirit renew your thoughts and attitudes.
                                        ~Ephesians 4:22-23 (NLT)

No, I can't do it," tears rolled down Carter's cheeks. "It's gonna hurt. I can't do it."

"Carter, your tooth is literally hanging on by a tiny piece of your gum. It's sticking out sideways. You have to pull it out. Come here and let me wiggle it." I reached over to wiggle his tooth.

"No, Mama. You're trying to trick me. You're gonna pull it," he covered his mouth with both hands. "Just don't touch it," he commanded through his fingers.

"I'm not going to pull it. I promise. I want to see how loose it is. Look. I will only touch it with one finger. There's no way I can grab it with one finger." He conceded. And boy was that tooth wiggly. No matter how I tried to convince him, he would not agree to let me pull the tooth.

Three hours later, after we ate a miserably long and whiny supper, he agreed to let my husband tie a piece of dental floss around it and pop it out. Helping David tie a tiny knot around a tiny tooth in Carter's tiny mouth was next to impossible with his giant bear-like hands. Finally, he got the dental floss tied securely on the tooth.

"One, two, THREE!" David pulled. And out popped the tooth.

"Is it out? Where is it? Am I done?"

"Yep, it's right here tied to the end of this string, just like a little pet tooth." We all laughed as Carter walked around with his tooth like a dog on a leash.

Carter was worried about the pain of getting rid of something that had always been there. He knew what his life was like with the tooth, but when it came time to deal with the tooth and get it out, he was afraid the pulling process would hurt too bad.

This sounds all too familiar. Just like Carter, we have had sins, habits, relationships, or attitudes in our lives for so long we are scared to let them go. Even though those areas and actions don't need to be there anymore, it's all we know, and to let go would mean forsaking all that is comfortable.

But just like Carter, we must reach a point where we pull that tooth out. Yes, the unknown future is scary, but holding onto junk instead of Jesus will cause a bunch more pain in the long run than simply pulling it out and taking a chance on Christ.

Do I have any teeth that are in the way that need to be pulled out so I can move forward into a fresh, pain free future?

Treed on the Couch

So humble yourselves before God. Resist the devil, and he will flee from you.

~James 4:7 (NLT)

All morning, the boys ran and chased each other through the house—wrestling, tackling, and jumping on everything. It was bad weather outside, so we were trapped.

I tried movies. Board games. Chores. Coloring. Drawing. Reading. Blocks. Trains. Cars. Nothing, I mean nothing would calm these two hooligans down, especially the little one.

"Alright. Enough," I declared. "Both of you. Go to your room and hit, punch, wrestle, fight, whatever you need to do to get it out of your system, but you can't do it in here. I'm done."

Both boys hung their heads and went into their room. Ten minutes later, Carter screamed, the bedroom door flew open, and Carter leapt onto the back of the couch. Daniel slid around the corner with some sort of plastic weapon, yelled like a wild man, and pointed it at Carter.

"Mama!" Cowering and covering his head, Carter screamed. "Make Daniel stop."

Honestly at this point I was stifling laughter. Here was my scrawny four-year-old who had my big eight-year-old treed like a squirrel on the back of my couch. "Carter, what is wrong with you? You have fifty pounds on this kid. Why are you the one treed on the back of the couch like a squirrel? Go get him!" The light suddenly came on, and off the couch he leaped, pillow in hand. Daniel ran screaming.

As I think about Carter, treed on the back of the couch, held captive by his little brother, I can't help but see the comparison to our own Christian lives. Instead of relying on God, we allow the enemy to turn the smaller issues of life into bigger ones, essentially treeing us on the back of the couch. We are unable to take a step forward, trapped by things that are insignificant in the kingdom of God. Fear, worry, anxiety, and stress pin us on the couch until we remember God has made us victorious over all that junk. If we stand up and resist, the enemy must flee. He doesn't have the control over our lives. God does.

What "little brothers" of this world have me treed and are holding me hostage on the back of the couch?

Buried Feet

Can all your worries add a single moment to your life?
~Matthew 6:27 (NLT)

Carter, I need your help holding the tape measure," I hollered across the front yard.

"Mama, I can't right now. I'm stuck," he sheepishly yelled back.

"Stuck? What in the world are you stuck on?"

"Not on. In," he replied.

As I rounded the corner, there stood Carter beside the swing with Daniel heaving dirt with a shovel onto Carter's feet.

"Carter's going to bury my feet next, but I'm doing his first," Daniel told me excitedly.

"I can definitely see why you can't help me," I snickered. "Just don't bury any whole bodies. Only feet."

As I thought about Carter's feet buried in the sand, I considered my own feet. Often nervous and unsteady, second guessing every step of the way. When big decisions need to be made, even when I know God is leading, I freeze.

It all boils down to control and trust. I want to be in control and I lack trust in God. I question His motives and try to figure out better options for my life. I think I know better. I. I. I. And the whole while, my feet are getting buried deeper and deeper in the ground of uncertainty, doubt, and faithlessness.

Are you bogged down in the sand? Maybe it's time to set that shovel down.

Do I trust God's direction or do I freeze, get stuck, and bury my feet in the sand?

Fishing Baseball

Be careful how you live. Don't live like fools, but like those who are wise. Make the most of every opportunity in these evil days.

~Ephesians 5:15-16 (NLT)

My husband has taught me a number of ways to beat the system. The boys needed to be pushed on the horse swing, but he wanted to work on something else while in the yard. He found an old rope, tied it in the tree, and now the boys hold it and pull themselves, almost like reins on a real horse.

Baseball was the same way. We got tired of chasing the ball across the yard when the boys hit it, so David got a fishing pole, tied a ball to the end of the line and duct-taped it real tight.

The first day we sat in the yard with a ball taped to the end of a fishing line, I thought David had lost his mind. But he held the pole out with the ball dangling. He told Carter to swing and as he hit the ball, he allowed the bale on the fishing pole to release. The fishing line sang like a trout was on the other end as the ball went down the hill. Instead of chasing it like we did before, all he had to do was reel it in. Fishing baseball quickly became our new favorite outside game.

My husband is all about working smarter, not harder. He strives to utilize his time but also reduce extra strain on his achy joints. His way of handling life reminds me of Paul's instructions to the Ephesians to make the most of their time because the days are so evil. God wants us to be wise in the way we conduct our lives. He wants us to work smarter, not harder, and pay attention to the world around us so we are able to continually represent Christ in the best way possible.

Is there anything I'm neglecting in my spiritual life that would help me work smarter and not harder to best represent Christ?

Popping the Chips

"So why do you keep calling me 'Lord, Lord!' when you don't do what I say?

~Luke 6:46 (NLT)

Mama, can I pop this bag of chips?" Daniel hollered from the back seat.

"No, you may not. Please open them correctly," I replied.

"But, Mama. I learned how at school from my friends and it opens the bag up so I can eat them if I pop it. Why not?"

"First, you are not popping that bag because I instructed you not to and that would mean you are disobeying. Second, when you pop a bag of chips, it can crush the chips and leave you with crumbs. Third, the bag makes a bunch of noise in this confined space. And fourth, the bag might pop in the wrong place and leave you covered in chips, not to mention my whole backseat as well. Don't pop the chips."

"Okay, fine. I don't want them right now. I will eat them later," he folded his arms and made his point, tossing the chips in the seat beside him.

A few minutes later, I passed the boys off to my parents. "Now Daniel has a snack when he is hungry. He never ate his chips from lunch," I told my dad.

Fast forward three hours. "Mama, I popped my chips in Papa's car," he giggled. "I couldn't help myself. I just wanted to so bad."

Daniel is just like us grown-ups. The sins we shouldn't partake in seem overly appealing. Our boundary lines and limits appear less defined and we just can't help ourselves. Justifications enter into the picture and before long we have popped that bag of chips and don't see anything wrong with it.

But God does. Every sin hurts His heart and moves us further away from Him. Every act of disobedience is a step in the wrong direction. Every time we pop those chips, we say no to God.

What areas have I been making justifications and allocations for sin?

Pay the Toll

He takes no pleasure in the strength of a horse or in human might. No, the LORD's delight is in those who fear him those who put their hope in his unfailing love.

~Psalm 147:10-11 (NLT)

My husband rocked our boys to sleep every night for the first four years of their lives. It was one of the best parts of his day getting to hold a little guy in his lap. During the waking hours, I got my chance to hold them while reading, napping, or watching television shows. There is nothing sweeter than little boy snuggles.

As the boys have gotten older, our laps are empty more often. I find myself bribing them to come sit with me or grabbing them when they walk by, pulling them into my lap. Even then, they don't stay as long. They are off to bigger things and don't want to snuggle with Mama as much anymore.

But I do get some sweet moments. I imposed a rule several years ago that if one of them needs something from me or wants to pass by, they have to pay the toll. The toll is simply a kiss on my cheek. Or on both cheeks. Whatever I feel at the moment. I tap my check and say, "Okay, you can get past me, but you have to pay the toll." Of course they oblige and it warms this mama's heart.

Just like my boys warm my heart with their sweet kisses and occasional snuggles, I, too, want to warm my Father's heart with the way that I live my life. Oh that I may bring a smile to His face and joy to His soul.

Am I living my life in such a way that I warm my Father's heart?

Acknowledgements

I would like to first thank my mom for encouraging me on this journey from the beginning. Your love of words is contagious and your belief in me, unwavering. Countless papers edited, conferences attended, and projects tackled. Thank you, Mom. And thank you, Dad, Granny, Papa, Carter, and Daniel for always reminding me to chase my dreams. David, you work so hard to provide for our family. Thank you for putting in the extra time so I can chase this crazy writing dream of mine. Vicki, you challenged me to take a whole day each week to write and then opened your home for me to use. Your encouragement and friendship mean more than you know.

Releah Lent and Sylvia Tomberlin, you two told me I was writer. Thank you for pushing me to chase my dreams. Cindy Sproles, thank you for believing in me at such a pivotal point in time. Beth Patch, you were the one who published my first devotion online. I'm so grateful you took a chance on this newbie.

Mike Parker, my publisher, thank you for believing in this project and going along with my suggestions and changes. I'm grateful for the privilege of making this devotional so personal.

Thank you, friends and readers. I am blessed to be supported and loved by such a wonderful tribe of caring individuals. As I am recalling so many faces, I am humbled to the point of tears. The outpouring of love and encouragement I receive from each one of you on a regular basis is overwhelming.

And thank you, God, for this gift of writing. Never in my life have I been so fulfilled as I have been while writing for you. My prayer is that you are honored with these words. Thank you.

About the Author

CHRISTY BASS ADAMS

Christy Bass Adams worked in education for 18 years and now serves as the Outreach and Connections Coordinator at Fellowship Baptist Church. She is passionate about connecting people within the Body of Christ and helping fellow believers find a place to serve and grow. Her writing career includes a weekly inspirational column for Greene Publishing and regular contributions to Vinewords.net and Inspireafire.com. Christy is a multi-award winner in a variety of literary categories as well as a contributor to two inspirational anthologies. Her most important role, however, is that of a wife, and mother to two busy, adventurous boys.

Christy's love for reading and writing was fueled first by her mother, and then by her middle and high school English teachers. These amazing humans exposed her to authors and literature that set her soul ablaze and stirred her ever growing imagination. With a natural bent toward encouraging others, Christy loves to share the life-giving breath of words with everyone she meets.

As God has so radically grown Christy in her walk with Him, she desires to share the hope of Christ with others she encounters on life's journey. If she can offer even a strand of hope to a hurting soul, her mission is accomplished.

For more about Christy, visit her online at:

www.christybassadams.com